Endorsements

"*Too Soon to Say Goodbye* is a life preserver for those drowning in the deep seas of suicide grief. The stories in this book acknowledge and validate the shifting thoughts and feelings of those grieving the loss of a loved one to suicide and provide a vision of life beyond this devastating loss."

—CANDY ARRINGTON, coauthor of *Aftershock: Help, Hope, and Healing in the Wake of Suicide*

"If you have suffered a loved one taking their life, you will want to read this book. It tackles the painful questions of those left behind asking why. My mother succeeded on her seventh attempt to take her own life. I was 12 when she made her first unsuccessful attempt. I was 27 when she succeeded. I wondered for 30 years why my brother and I were not a sufficient reason for my mother to want to live. I wish someone could have given me *Too Soon to Say Goodbye* to help me understand how better to deal with the hurt that followed. This book, along with your love, would be the best gift you could give a friend whose loved one has chosen to believe the lie that suicide is the best answer to their desperation."

—GARY RICHMOND, author of *The Divorce Decision*

Too Soon to Say Goodbye

HEALING *and* HOPE *for* VICTIMS *and* SURVIVORS *of* SUICIDE

Susan Titus Osborn, MA
Karen L. Kosman
Jeenie Gordon, MS, MA, LMFT

NEW HOPE
PUBLISHERS
Birmingham, Alabama

New Hope® Publishers
P. O. Box 12065
Birmingham, AL 35202-2065
www.newhopepublishers.com

New Hope Publishers is a division of WMU®.

Library of Congress Cataloging-in-Publication Data

Osborn, Susan Titus, 1944-
  Too soon to say goodbye : healing and hope for victims and
survivors of suicide / Susan Titus Osborn, Karen Kosman, Jeenie Gordon.
    p. cm.
  ISBN 978-1-59669-243-5 (sc)
  1. Consolation. 2. Suicide--Religious aspects--Christianity. I.
Kosman, Karen L., 1942- II. Gordon, Jeenie. III. Title.
  BV4905.3.O83 2010
  248.8'68--dc22
                        2009033390

All Scripture quotations, unless otherwise noted, are taken from the HOLY BIBLE, NEW INTERNATIONAL VERSION®. NIV®. Copyright © 1973, 1978, 1984 by International Bible Society. Used by permission of Zondervan. All rights reserved.

Scripture quotations marked (*The Message*) are taken from *The Message* by Eugene H. Peterson. Copyright © 1993, 1994, 1995, 1996, 2000, 2001, 2002. Used by permission of NavPress Publishing Group.

Scripture quotations marked (KJV) are taken from The Holy Bible, King James Version.

Scripture quotations marked (NLT) are taken from the *Holy Bible*, New Living Translation, copyright © 1996. Used by permission of Tyndale House Publishers, Inc., Wheaton, Illinois. All rights reserved.

Cover design: Left Coast, www.lcoast.com
Interior design: Sherry Hunt

ISBN-10: 1-59669-243-X
ISBN-13: 978-1-59669-243-5

N094138 · 0110 · 3M1

For Karen's son, Robbie,
who died due to suicide at the age of 23.

And for all the Robbies of the world,
young and old, male and female.

Table of Contents

The first reaction that follows the news of a loved one's suicide is overwhelming denial. "Denial" screams out against reality. The initial shock wave washes over the survivor's mind and shouts, *This can't be true! It must be a mistake!*

Those who have lost someone to suicide struggle to understand why death was chosen over life. The haunting question of why torments surviving family members.

Anger, abandonment, shame, and guilt are just a few of the feelings that bombard those who have lost someone to suicide. How does one live with the pain and stigma of suicide? Does one ever feel "good" again?

The person struggling with suicidal thoughts needs to have support and understanding. Even with well-meaning friends and family, the suicidal individual needs professional care.

Even though the pain greatly lessens with time and people go on with their lives, there will always be residual pain. Eventually there needs to come a sense of closure—and peace.

Rarely is there a person in the throes of divorce who does not have the thought cross her mind, *I don't want to live through this*. If suicide occurs, a ripple effect flows through the family left behind.

CHAPTER 7: *God, Help Me!*   107

Not seeing a life preserver or other means of escape, a person can quickly sink into a watery abyss. That's exactly what happens when we have no solid anchor in life—Christ. As with a life preserver, we must allow Him to encompass us, help us to relax, and carry us to safety.

CHAPTER 8: *On the Edge*   121

When a person has had suicidal thoughts, it is important for her to find someone to talk to—a friend, pastor, or family therapist. Most suicides are split-second decisions. If suicide thoughts are dealt with early on, we can save lives.

CHAPTER 9: *Saving a Life*   137

Those who have attempted suicide may daily face the need for medication, counseling, and in some cases, the fear that depression might win out over their desire to live. There are times when intervention from a friend or family member makes a difference and saves a life.

CHAPTER 10: *Forgiveness: The Path to Freedom*   153

Forgiveness often lies many years down the road. But forgiveness is a commandment, not a suggestion. Our heavenly Father knows the freedom that forgiveness will bring into a shattered life.

Every step forward in returning to normalcy takes courage. The individual or grieving family must face the stigma and rejection that accompanies a death by suicide and find courage in the Lord to go on.

Once again, life takes on purpose, and God's sovereignty provides hope even in darkness. Life no longer is taken for granted. Every moment is precious.

A LETTER TO ROBBIE

"For I know the plans I have for you," declares the Lord, "plans to prosper you and not to harm you, plans to give you hope and a future. Then you will call upon me and come and pray to me, and I will listen to you."
—Jeremiah 29:11–12

Twenty-four years after Karen's son, Robbie, took his own life, she wrote him a letter—a letter already written for many years on her heart. It includes sorrow, love, healing, and a mother's eternal hope. Revealed in this letter is a promise to Robbie to reach out to others contemplating suicide, as well as to families who are suffering its aftermath.

Dear Robbie,

I want you to know how much I miss you. I'll never understand why you decided to leave. If only you had told us how much you were hurting. Did you really believe no one cared?

The police said they found no suicide note—just a story that you wrote about a boy in the fifth grade, a boy ten years old, whose parents were divorced and remarried. The situation made him feel there was no place to go. The police didn't understand, but I did. I shed many tears over that story. Ten is how old you were when your sister died. I remember how depressed her death made you feel. Had you become emotionally stuck at 10? Had you not moved on?

Twenty-four years have passed since you said goodbye, and yet in the stillness of the night I hold dear my memories of the little boy you once were. The boy with the big questioning eyes—eyes that always looked so sad when someone made fun of your speech impediment. Sometimes they reflected a pain too deep for crying. I also remember how they sparkled at times with mischief and other times with merriment. I loved the freckles across your nose and that stubborn cowlick that would not lie down.

The imprint of your small 4-year-old hand was one of the best presents anyone gave me. I know how hard school was for you. Did you ever understand that children with learning disabilities are not dumb? They just learn differently!

Do you remember the Christmas right after your 18th birthday? The budget was tight that year, and I truly thought we wouldn't be able to afford a tree. Then on Christmas Eve you walked through the front door carrying a six-foot tree. You smiled and said, "Mom, I worked at a Christmas tree lot and earned this tree." I'd never been more proud of you.

You had such determination, Robbie. When you worked for your Uncle Roy, I marveled at the distance you traveled on your motorcycle.

Each year on your birthday, I stop and ponder what you may have become. What wonderful accomplishments you would have achieved if you'd chosen to stay. I wonder if you would have married and how many grandchildren you'd have given me. I'll never know—you went away too soon. I miss your hugs. You always seemed to know when I needed one. I miss your smile; it always brightened my day.

I felt a lot of anger when you left. It's hard not knowing why you chose to leave. God impressed on my heart that I could be bitter, feel guilty, and show anger, or I could let go of those emotions—not with my own strength, but with His.

*I love you, Robbie, which will never change. But when
I stand at your gravesite, I can't put my arms around you
anymore. I have so many sweet memories, but I don't have you
anymore. At holidays and special moments with family, there is
always an empty chair.*

*I am sharing your life and death with others in hopes that it
prevents someone else's son or daughter, mom or dad, or friend or
relative from dying by suicide.*

*I know, if you could, you'd tell people that no matter how
difficult life seems, it will get better. You always learned through
trial and error. Robbie, your life had purpose, and I know that
your suicide was your ultimate act of impulsiveness—but at what
cost. . . .*

Love,
Mom

The fact that you are reading this book probably means you are
someone who has been touched in some way by suicide. Perhaps
you've lost a loved one or friend to suicide. Maybe at some time in
your life you were suicidal, or you know someone who is extremely
depressed. In these pages you'll find stories shared by people* who
have walked where you are now. These are ordinary people who
have overcome the darkness that invaded their lives. Once again
light shines for them, and it can for you, too.

*Many of the names in this book and some details have been changed to protect the
privacy of these individuals.

For Those Left Behind
Charles R. Brown

Death comes veiled in tragedy's mask
even when we anticipate an aged patriarch's passing.
But the loss is magnified
when a friend or loved one gives up
and pushes the button to escape the suffering.

At times like this
we sit and stare at the floor.
How, dear God, should we pray?
Our hearts ache. Our minds are crammed with why.
Sleep seems to come only with restless exhaustion.
But You, Lord, know start to finish.
Somehow let us find re*creation* in Your completeness.
As we cherish good memories
remind us to intercede often for the children,
the friends, and the family that must continue the journey here.
We ask, too, that You would bring
refreshment from this bitter drink.
Bathe the grieving with words from You,
words of comfort and hope.
Through this unwanted stealing away,
bring the abundance of Your sufficiency.
We pray this for Your glory
in the name of our Savior.
Amen

CHAPTER 1

"PLEASE, GOD, THIS MUST BE A MISTAKE"

There is a time for everything,
and a season for every activity under heaven:
a time to be born and a time to die,
a time to plant and a time to uproot,
a time to kill and a time to heal,
a time to tear down and a time to build.
—Ecclesiastes 3:1–3

All of us, with surety, will someday die. Nevertheless, we plan to reach a ripe old age before we face death. There seems to be an appropriateness that surrounds the face of death due to old age.

Many of us have also experienced the loss of a loved one. And we've felt the pain of *grief*—the process we all must go through to find eventual acceptance. We are not speaking of mourning over the actual event, but rather the beginning of a belief we will someday be all right in spite of the absence of this loved one. In time, we begin to move ahead with our lives, finding comfort in the hope and assurance that God offers.

Yet, there is a type of loss that is much less easily accepted. That is the loss of a loved one through suicide. The painful knowledge someone dear to us has chosen to end his or her life causes an overwhelming agony. Our minds plead with God, *Please, this must be a mistake.* Mind, body, and soul diligently grapple for a means to escape from the devastating pain, but there is no escape from the reality of suicide. For the individual or family left behind, suicide is a time when faith is tested beyond any human reasoning.

In order to have a deeper understanding of suicide and its aftermath, we must be willing to share the pain of those individuals and families who have lost a loved one through suicide. Grief affects not only the physical body and mind, but the soul as well. King David expresses this in Psalm 31:9: *"Be merciful to me, O Lord, for I am in distress; my eyes grow weak with sorrow, my soul and my body with grief."*

In order to better understand the pain suicide survivors experience, this chapter focuses on stories of initial shock, disbelief, and grief. But this chapter also tells of profound hope found in the midst of sorrow.

In the following story Karen is touched by the loss of a friend's son through suicide. She never imagined that someday she'd understand the depth of that loss in a personal way.

The Painful Silence
Karen Kosman

For 14 years I worked in the medical laboratory of a hospital. As I daily walked down hospital corridors, I heard hurrying feet, wheelchairs, gurneys, elevator bells, and overhead pages vibrate with energy and urgency. Then there were the sounds of the human voices chattering, crying, and laughing, while others slipped into total silence.

The hospital for me remained an emotionally fast-paced world—a place where life and death played out daily. There were times when I needed to steal a few minutes of calm, maybe outside on the patio, under the shade of a tree, or in the hospital chapel. Our break room offered a combination of both solitude and friendly talk among co-workers. Usually it was a happy place.

Perhaps that's why I noticed the painful silence as I entered the lounge one afternoon. No one even looked up when I walked in. As I glanced from face to face, I saw sadness and teary eyes. When I couldn't stand the silence anymore, I asked, "What's wrong?"

"Melanie's 14-year-old son, Chuck, took his life last night," Nancy said in a barely audible voice.

Suddenly, I felt the need to breathe in deeply, as if my body had the air sucked out of it.

"Oh, my! Why?"

"No one knows. He left a note that said, 'Life is too painful.'"

As medical personnel, we had all, at one time or other, witnessed the pain of suicide. But this was too close to home. This affected someone we personally knew and worked with.

That night I returned home drained, but felt relieved when I found my own teenagers alive and well. The next day the newspaper had an article and picture of Chuck. He had hung himself. As I gazed upon Chuck's image, a handsome young man whose life had ended too soon, I wondered why.

There had been another time in my life when a high school classmate had taken his own life. I felt shocked and terrified that someone so young could take his own life. The same sense of bewilderment plagued me in this present situation.

Melanie took a leave of absence for a month. When she returned to work, she seemed to function at her job as a medical technician, but remained distant and silent about what had happened. Anyone who looked into Melanie's pain-filled eyes knew they were seeing a part of her soul that they could not share. The one comment I often heard Melanie make, "I keep waiting to wake up and find out this is a mistake," haunted me.

Many times I wanted to hug Melanie and ask how she was, but I hesitated and kept silent. Like everyone else, I didn't want to say or do anything that would open the floodgate to her hurtful memories.

The only explanation we heard about Chuck's suicide was he suffered from low self-esteem. Soon the talk about what happened diminished, and we all resumed our own lives. We were grateful to go home to our kids and our problems, which did not include losing a loved one due to suicide.

Lack of understanding kept us from embracing and listening to someone whose life had been turned inside out. By avoiding the subject of Chuck's suicide, we all remained prisoners—in a painful silence that only sharing could heal.

Four years later, with the death of my own son by suicide, I found myself experiencing what my friend Melanie had. When I returned to work after my son's death, Melanie embraced me and said, "If you need to talk, I'm here for you."

Tears filled my eyes, for I'd learned within the three short weeks after my loss how valuable friends were who broke the barrier of silence. Because Melanie had been there, she was able to embrace my pain and listen to my heart.

As we must render an account of every idle word, so we must of our idle silence.
—Ambrose of Milan

☼ ☼ ☼

The pain of suicide is like a jigsaw puzzle with a missing piece. No matter how we try, we cannot make the pieces fit together. Without that missing piece, called understanding, we feel helpless.

We can't expect friends to provide answers to our bewilderment. Most of them don't know what a suicide survivor is going through and don't know what to say. Their silence is not meant to hurt, but is a sign of their own discomfort. Depending on how close they were to the deceased person, it may be a sign of their own grief.

As I work in therapy with clients who are experiencing great emotional trauma, they often express Melanie's thoughts: "I keep waiting to wake up and find out this is a mistake."

Elisabeth Kübler-Ross, who did extensive work on healing from the death of a loved one, describes steps in the healing process. The first step is denial. "I can't believe this is happening…it's a terrible nightmare…I'll wake up from this," etc. One of the first reactions is that of disbelief. A person's emotions are in shock mode and are unable to accept the horrific event; thus, denial is a normal and vital part of the eventual recovery process.

Denial is imperative to the grieving process. It allows the physical body to absorb the shock of the loss. It helps us move through the motions of notifying family and friends and making funeral arrangements.

GRIEVING TOGETHER

So, what can be done in the face of grief and denial? There is One who understands the trauma of grief, as well as the accompanying sorrow and disappointment when friends don't understand. Read about Jesus's agonizing night in Matthew 26:36–46. When Jesus came to the garden of Gethsemane to pray, His heart ached with fear and anxiety over what lay ahead for Him—the Cross.

He chose not to go to the garden alone. His disciples went with Him. In Matthew 26:38 Jesus said to them, *"My soul is overwhelmed with sorrow even unto the point of death. Stay here and keep watch with me."* Then Jesus went off alone to pray.

"Then he returned to his disciples and found them sleeping. 'Could you men not keep watch with me for one hour?' he asked Peter" (Matthew 26:40).

Even in His distress Jesus openly expressed His feelings to His friends. We see in Jesus the need for compassion, fellowship, and prayer. No one should have to endure sorrow alone. You can reach out. A friend who shares another's grief helps to carry a portion of that person's sorrow.

How vividly Jeenie remembers a family who came to her office following their daughter's tragic death and burial a few days before. Listening to their story and observing their heartbreak, Jeenie sat and wept with them. Following the session, she berated herself for not being therapeutic. She could only cry.

In subsequent sessions, however, Jeenie was able to counsel them. At the end of therapy, the mother stated, "That first day when you sat and cried with us, we knew we had the right therapist."

If Jesus needed His disciples so desperately in His time of inexpressible grief, how much more do we need support? And, when we grieve with those who hurt, we are pleasing to God.

With a mother's heart, Karen shares the pain she felt at the news of her own son's suicide. In her own words, "The foundation of my life turned to quicksand, and I didn't know if I'd be able to find a solid basis once again to stabilize my faith. Although 24 years have passed, the vividness of that night is as real as if it were yesterday."

"I Love You, Robbie"
Karen Kosman

After an afternoon of Christmas shopping with my daughter, Linda, we returned home. Struggling with our arms full of packages, we stepped on the front porch. Suddenly the front door opened, and my husband, John, stood in the entrance looking pale. I sensed something terribly wrong—a horrific foreboding raced through me.

John's eyes were filled with tears as he gently said, "Karen, we had a phone call from Tacoma."

Immediately I thought of my son. "Robbie phoned?" I asked.

"No, it was about Robbie."

"Is he all right? Is he sick? Did he have an accident?"

"Karen, they found him in his apartment dead."

Those words pierced my heart like a flaming arrow. "No! No! No! It's a mistake. My son is coming home for Christmas! The whole family chipped in to bring him home. It's his Christmas gift. John, you know that this has to be a mistake!"

"Honey," John said trembling, "the police called. It's not a mistake. His landlord hadn't seen him and thought he'd better check on him. He found Robbie's body."

I collapsed against my husband for support. "What happened?" I whispered.

"Karen, I know how painful this is. Robbie was my stepson, but I loved him as if he were my own." John sighed. "Karen, he died by suicide."

I heard the words, but my mind searched for a way to escape. I looked at the front door and prayed, *Please, God, this must be a mistake.* But the silence in the room closed in, and I felt strangely alone with my heartbeat echoing inside my head. It beat so hard my temples pulsated. When the shock settled in, I felt numb. I looked at my husband and saw sorrow etched on his face. John nodded his head as if he understood. I walked over to the phone and dialed Robbie's dad.

"Ted, it's me, Karen." I hesitated, tears welling in my eyes. Then not knowing how to start, I sobbed, "Robbie…"

"I know. I got a phone call from Tacoma, too. I can't believe it," he said with the heaviness of regret in his voice. "Tomorrow we need to start making arrangements."

"Yes, OK," I replied, numbed and fighting my tears. Ted and I said goodbye, and Linda walked over to me. She threw her arms around me, and we cried together. Just a few hours earlier Linda and I were Christmas shopping, anticipating a Christmas shared with Robbie. How quickly our lives had changed.

Later that night, I lay awake thinking of my son. Life

had never been easy for Robbie. My labor had been long and difficult. Oxygen deprivation at birth led to developmental problems for Robbie as he grew up—a speech disorder, learning disabilities, and a hearing perception problem. At the age of 20, dyslexia was finally diagnosed. In addition to Robbie's other problems, he was impulsive. He would often take action before thinking things through.

Robbie moved from our home in California to Oregon at the age of 22. He wanted to prove to himself that he could make it on his own. But he had irresponsibly left a special training program that would have placed him with a company willing to work with his special needs.

"Robbie," I pleaded, "please finish your program."

"Mom, don't worry. My friends in Portland will help me find a job."

John and I had taken him to the bus depot. At six feet tall, Robbie towered over me. When he hugged me, I rested my head against his chest, not wanting to let go.

"Mom, I'll be fine," he said reassuringly. I looked into his brown eyes, sparkling with hope.

"I love you, Robbie."

A month later, the promised job fell through, and he'd traveled to Tacoma, Washington. Soon he found a job and established himself in a home church. When he got his own apartment he felt so proud. It had seemed to all of us back home in California that he would be OK. We were so happy for him. But now, one phone call shattered all my hopes and dreams of a happy future for my son. That night tears soaked my pillow, and finally I slipped into fretful sleep.

In the middle of the night, I woke up trembling, and in the stillness I prayed, *Please, Lord, help me.* Then a verse came to mind. *"Jesus wept"* (John 11:35). From that moment on, I knew I would not be alone in my grief. Somewhere within the depths of my heart stood a Cross, and I knew that God Himself understood my grief.

⚡ ⚡ ⚡

Karen's story is not just about grief, but also of an eternal hope and a heavenly Father whose wings wrapped around her heart and never left. God taught Karen through her tears about the power behind His promise: *"Never will I leave you; never will I forsake you"* (Hebrews 13:5).

In the next story, Terri Evans believed that the "danger" for her son had passed. But the truth is that none of us have the ability to see into the future. Nor do we have the ability to get inside the person we love and find out what he or she is feeling and thinking.

Sometimes circumstances and actions raise a red flag, indicating that all is not well. We seek help. We sit through therapy sessions and allow the use of medications. We encourage. Yet, we still have to let go. No matter how much we love our depressed children, or other loved ones, their choices are not always within our control. Often the fatal choice is discovered too late.

Terri's story, though heartrending, is also one of hope for healing and comfort in the midst of shock and grief.

"You Are Special"
Terri Evans

One spring day, I dressed and left for work. I didn't have a chance to say goodbye to my 16-year-old son Sean that morning.

Every parent wants clouds with silver linings for their children. My husband and I certainly wanted secure, happy lives for our two sons, Bryce and Sean. But something had gone terribly wrong for Sean.

For two years our family struggled in a life-and-death drama to save Sean from whatever tortured him. Our son was hospitalized for depression and diagnosed as bipolar. Sean made good progress in therapy. He'd acted happy and calmer.

During our family gatherings, Sean interacted with each of us. And in the last six months he'd grown exceptionally close to me. I used to tell him, "You will always be my boy." No matter how old he got or what happened, I would always love him and do my best to take care of him.

I wanted to believe that counseling, the diagnosis of bipolar disorder, and treatment with the proper medication had stabilized Sean—that we had our son back.

On the way to work that morning, I hoped Sean would be OK. My mind filled with thoughts. *It's a good sign that Sean has remained active in the youth group. Although he sleeps too much and still shows some signs of depression, he's going to make it, and so are we.*

My thoughts returned me to the present as I drove into the church lot. I parked the car and got out. What a blessing it was to work for the church that my family attended. Our church family had been very supportive during our struggles with Sean. The warmth of the sun felt reassuring as I walked toward the office. *Sean, please be OK today,* I silently prayed.

Later, I tried calling home to check on him, but there was no answer. *Sean, where are you? Did you go with a friend and forget to call me?* After work I drove straight home and entered the house through the garage door. The stillness sent a chill through me. "Sean!" I called. But only silence replied.

Heading down the hallway to Sean's room I felt my heart racing. Sean's bedroom door was shut. *Maybe he's asleep.* Usually, I'd find Sean reading, playing video games, sitting at the computer, or outside working on homework at the picnic bench with his headphones on. As I neared his room, I felt an overwhelming sense of dread. I placed my hand on the doorknob and opened it.

"Sean, noooo!"

When I saw him, I knew he'd never wake up again. He had taken his life.

A short time later, my house vibrated with many voices. I went through the motions of answering questions for the coroner, although I felt numb inside.

An elder from church arrived to comfort me, and other church friends came to be with me. My husband worked 45 minutes away, and I anxiously awaited his arrival. Trapped within my own thoughts, I vaguely realized what was going on around me. *Sean is only 16. It's too soon to say goodbye. If only I'd wake up from this nightmare to find it has been a bad dream.*

Over the next few days I closed my eyes and tried to picture Sean in the arms of Jesus. "God, I don't understand. I thought You were answering our prayers. I thought Sean was getting well!" I cried.

Our church family remained very supportive to my family. They helped us with a beautiful memorial service. Sean's youth group put together a video of Sean's life. Memories of our son were shared. Scripture, prayer, and songs brought us to the foot of the Cross, where our hearts prayed for acceptance and a renewal of hope.

※ ※ ※

Words from Jeenie

Many times in my therapy practice people tell me how they have had a premonition that something bad was about to happen. Throughout Sean's last day on earth, his mother had a sense something was amiss. Thus, she did not knock on Sean's bedroom door, which would have probably been her pattern. I believe God often prepares us for forthcoming trauma. It's part of His loving-kindness.

Suicide, in my professional opinion, is carried out in a moment of insanity—clear thinking has ceased. The enormity of pain is at the center. In their muddled thinking, relief can only be achieved by ending life.

Sean's family will always think of him. As healing eventually emerges, memories of the lovely and beautiful will become stronger. And, the knowledge that Sean is with His Savior will be dominant. Therein lies eternal hope.

Peg Rose wanted to reach out to her neighbor, Terri Evans. Peg's son, Josh, had known Sean since grade school. Attending Sean's funeral, Peg prayed she'd be able to offer comfort. Yet to her surprise, she came away from Sean's funeral feeling ministered to and refreshed.

Standing Firm

Peggy Matthews Rose

"I just wondered if Josh knew what time the funeral service is tomorrow," said the young man at the door. He'd come looking for our son, who was not home.

"Service for whom?" I asked.

"For Sean."

"Sean?" *Surely he couldn't mean Sean Evans.* "Sean Evans?" I asked.

"Yes. I thought you knew."

What my family hadn't known until that surrealistic moment was that Sean Evans, the younger brother of our son's childhood playmate, Bryce, had taken his own life just a few days earlier. As often happens when kids grow into adulthood, Josh and Bryce had drifted apart during their teen years. Though we were neighbors and fellow believers, life and its excuse of busyness had kept the Evanses and the Roses from ever becoming more than the parents of childhood chums. We didn't know them well.

Still—I was stunned. How could this happen? It couldn't be true! Hadn't Sean been a toddler in diapers just the other day? Hadn't he been his older brother's constant companion when playing at our house with our son? Wasn't he the one most likely to be the best and brightest on the block? We saw him walk by now and then and marked the constantly changing hairstyles that were common to his generation. But we'd had no knowledge of the bipolar world Sean lived and suffered in.

I went to his memorial service expecting a far different scene from the one I witnessed. Such a devastating loss would undoubtedly produce grieving beyond belief and the screaming question of why. Instead, I saw a place filled with life, hope, and love, as Mark and Terri Evans showed their friends and neighbors what it means to be Christians.

Whatever happens, conduct yourselves in a manner worthy of the gospel of Christ. Then, whether I come and see you or only hear about you in my absence, I will know that you stand firm in one spirit, contending as one man for the faith of the gospel without being frightened in any way by those who oppose you.
—Philippians 1:27–28

These precious grieving parents brought these words, spoken by the Apostle Paul almost 2,000 years ago, to life.

No one can escape the reality of death. Funerals serve to remind us of that fact. But where we spend our life after death *is* a choice. The enemy of Christ strives to deceive us regarding this choice, but regardless this is a choice we must make here and now.

In their grief, Sean's parents offered a message of hope. At Sean's funeral the pastor spoke of heaven as a place for those prepared to go, and an invitation to receive Christ was given. Concerned that no one leave that solemn place without hope for their own future, these parents offered a Bible to anyone attending who did not have one. Through Christ, they were standing firm in the face of tragedy.

☀ ☀ ☀

No one knows what tomorrow will bring, but we can trust One who will carry us safely through it. You, too, can know this hope, the hope of Christ. It's the same hope that carried Terri's family through this horrific ordeal of grief and continues to enable them to face each day without seeing Sean grow into manhood, become a husband, or give them grandchildren.

Why did he do it? Only God really knows. Likely even Sean would not be able to give a reason. He was just reacting to internal pain. Could it have been prevented? Perhaps, but that also is a question only God can answer. What matters now is what God can do, and is doing, through the family left behind.

If you have lost a loved one to suicide, God is giving you an opportunity to come to His outstretched arms for comfort, healing, and peace. Only He knows the depth of our sorrow.

REFLECTIONS

1. Name the emotions your heart and mind are screaming.

2. Besides God, whom can you cry with? If you believe you have no one, ask God to bring someone to you. It may be a person you do not expect, but God knows your need.

3. When you feel a need to cry—cry. Take a few minutes to be by yourself and allow the tears to flow. Do not squelch them. Tears help the healing process.

Prayer

O Lord! My heart is broken. I feel so powerless, so hopeless. I need Your help. I need Your presence. In Jesus's name I pray, amen.

CHAPTER 2

WHY?

"Can you fathom the mysteries of God?
Can you probe the limits of the Almighty?"
—Job 11:7

Wonderful memories fill many of our minds as we watch children explore their surroundings. Children are filled with insatiable curiosity as they point and ask, "What's that, Mommy?" Eyes grow large with wonder, and even after many explanations, they'll still ask the question, "Why?"

After we become adults we continue to search and ponder the whys of life. Our world is full of technical questions about gadgets because of our innate need to explore and try to understand the mysteries of science. We live in a world where significant advances in medical research have given answers to many questions, especially in the fight against diseases. We can handle pain and illness better when we are given a logical explanation for suffering.

Yet as much as we want an answer to why our loved one has chosen suicide, we may never know the reason. It is seemingly a great mystery as to why anyone would choose death over life. Yet, according to the American Foundation of Suicide Prevention, more than 33,000 people per year in the United States die from suicide. For each person who dies, there are many other people who are profoundly affected.

Family and friends of the deceased are known as *suicide survivors*. They are left pondering why. *"Why didn't I realize something was wrong? "Why did God allow this to happen?" "Why didn't she ask for help?"* Like an echo, these questions reverberate against the walls of each survivor's heart until they are sure it will shatter into a million pieces.

The following quote describes behavior we can all identify with:

> One of the most tragic things I know about human nature is that all of us tend to put off living. We are all dreaming of some magical rose garden over the horizon—instead of enjoying the roses that are blooming outside our windows today.
> —Dale Carnegie

In an extreme sense, something similar happens to those who are suicidal. People who contemplate suicide have lost the ability to reach outside of their minds to ask for help. They have forgotten how to touch, how to cry, and even how to laugh. They do not really want to die, only to escape the pain that rages within them. Suicidal thoughts, like weeds, block their ability to enjoy the beauty that surrounds them. They have become imprisoned in their own minds with the inability to work through destructive thoughts.

When they choose the avenue of suicide, again we ask, "Why?"

MARY AND MARTHA ASK WHY

In John 11:1–35, the story of the death and raising of Lazarus, we discover all the questions that usually accompany a time of mourning. In this story, ordinary people, just like us, questioned why something tragic happened.

Imagine the scene the day Lazarus died. Heaviness must have weighed on the hearts and minds of his family and friends, causing confusion and doubt. Mary and Martha huddled together—their bodies trembling, tears falling, questions raging. *Why did Jesus ignore us? Didn't He heal the lepers, the blind, and the demon-possessed? Why then had He allowed our brother, Lazarus, to die?* How Mary and Martha ached to understand. *Why had Jesus not come when they asked Him to?* Lazarus had been in the tomb for four days, so now it was too late!

When Martha saw Jesus approaching the village, she ran to meet Him.

> *"Lord," Martha said to Jesus, "If you had been here, my brother would not have died. But I know that even now God will give you whatever you ask."*
>
> *Jesus said to her, "Your brother will rise again."*
>
> *Martha answered, "I know he will rise again in the resurrection at the last day."*
>
> *Jesus said to her, "I am the resurrection and the life. He who believes in me will live, even though he dies, and whoever lives and believes in me will never die. Do you believe this?"*
>
> *"Yes, Lord," she told him, "I believe that you are the Christ, the Son of God, who was to come into the world."*

—John 11:21–27

In her time of grief, God's grace washed over Martha, lifting her from the dark pit of sorrow into the light of God's truth. Her heart must have been filled to overflowing when she went back to the house to get her sister, Mary.

As friends watched Mary get up and leave, many followed, thinking she was going to Lazarus' tomb. They did not want her to be alone in her grief. When Mary approached Jesus, she could not conceal her sorrow, her disappointment, and her anger. She knelt at His feet and cried.

"Lord, if you had been here, my brother would not have died" (John 11:32).

When Jesus saw her pain and suffering, His spirit became troubled. Even knowing that in a short time He would call Lazarus forth from the grave—Jesus wept.

Do you see yourself through the doubts, disappointments, and questions of Martha and Mary? *God, where were You? Why didn't You intervene?*

Isn't it possible that Jesus wept beside you as you stood by your loved one's grave?

In this world we may not get an answer to our whys or understand His purposes in our grief. But we can be assured that His grace is poured out on us, just as it was on Mary and Martha. Just as He personally knows your name; He knew the name of your loved one.

In this chapter several mothers and a brother search for an answer to the question of why. Although they find no decisive answer, they develop courage and perseverance to move forward after the suicide of their loved ones. They find ways to deal with their grief.

Nancy Palmer found herself battling to get help for her son. But 30-year-old Jason insisted that he did not need help. In her heart, Nancy knew that Jason, despite his statement, was headed down a road of no return. She felt helpless when he stormed out of the house.

The Club No One Wants to Join
Nancy J. Palmer

I belong to a club no one wants to join. Its membership is too costly—the death of a child.

I closed my journal after writing these words. My mind reflected once more on that day my life changed forever.

I have always loved the peacefulness of early morning, as sunlight breaks through the clouds and people begin their days. Yet on January 8, 2003, at six thirty in the morning, I struggled against a deep foreboding, which had enveloped my entire being—an uneasiness about my son, Jason, When the doorbell rang several hours later, I did not want to open the door.

My 30-year-old son had been living with us for several months. The previous night we'd had an argument. I knew that he suffered from a deep depression. Finally, I had confronted him and pleaded, "Jason, no one loves you as much as I do. Please get help!"

"I don't need help! I'm outta here!" he shouted as he stomped off to his room to pack.

Jason had become skillful at hiding his inner turmoil from friends and family, but I knew all the signs of Jason's depression. He had struggled on and off most of his life. The intensity of his emotional state this time frightened me. No matter how much my husband, Bill, our sons Bill III and Geoffrey, and I cared, we could not control Jason's choices. He needed professional help, and he had to be the one willing to seek it.

A Christian psychologist had provided me with a list of therapists that Jason could see, but he refused. Jason was separated from his son, Elijah, and his son's mother. She didn't know how to deal with Jason's depression and had left him. Jason's 3-year-old, autistic son certainly needed his daddy. I hoped and prayed that Elijah would be the reason Jason might change his mind and seek help.

Wandering into Jason's room after he left, I felt shocked to find his most cherished belongings—items he'd never left behind before. I tried to convince myself that he'd be back, that he'd announce, "Mom, I am ready to seek help."

The insistent ringing of the doorbell finally broke through my resolve not to answer the door. A chill ran down my spine as I faced a man I did not know. Suddenly, my eyes fell on Jason's driver's license attached to the stranger's clipboard. My heart sank, and I knew even before he asked the question, "Mrs. Palmer, do you know a Jason Palmer?"

"Yes, he's my son."

"We have some bad news. May we come in to speak with you?"

Inside my mind agonized, *Nooooo! Just go away!*

With no way of erasing the dreaded news, I invited the man and his female companion inside.

"This morning a woman heard a noise. When she investigated, she found Jason's body in a park. He shot himself."

I went into shock and felt strangely detached. I heard a hysterical woman crying, "Not my baby, not my son. Oh, Jason, Why? Why would you leave your loved ones? Why would you leave Elijah?"

Suddenly I realized the hysterical woman was me. Reality hit. Jason would not be coming home.

Today I still don't have an answer to my question, "Why?"

Yet I have found a renewal of hope by volunteering for a ministry on suicide prevention. This gives me a reason to keep going. I work with the knowledge that we cannot stop all suicides, but saving just one life is worth the effort. I speak whenever possible and tell young people about mental illness and that it's OK to ask for help.

Am I still grieving? Absolutely! Some days I wonder how I can go on. I miss Jason so much. Yet, I have my sons Bill III and Geoffrey, grandchildren, and a family whom I love. I know that God is walking next to me in my grief. He has brought two other mothers into my life who have lost sons, Terri Evans and Patti Zingaro. Although we live within a few miles of one another and have some of the same friends, we never met until our tragedies brought us together.

Now in a united effort, we work to reach out and help others. And although none of us has found an answer to our "Why?"—we see God making a difference.

My son wrote this poem sometime before his death.

A LONELY PATH
Jason Palmer

I marvel at the way you see my life and yours.
Do you understand what it is to be?
We are nothing alike but exactly the same.
Your laughter brings me to tears.
Can you taste them?
Are we not on the same journey,
Wherever our paths may lead?
Do not fear me,
Just accept me and hold my hand.

Words from Jeenie

Bargaining, according to Kübler-Ross, is another step in the healing process following trauma. It is normal to think such thoughts as: *If only I would have called a psychiatric hospital and had them put him on a 72-hour hold, they could have helped him.* Or, *If I had driven him to see a therapist instead of giving him the telephone number.* Or, *Why didn't I follow him when he left the house?*

In bargaining, we try to think of ways we could have changed the outcome. So, there are scores of if onlys. It is not uncommon to bargain with God: "I'll do anything You ask." We make extreme vows—again, hoping to change the devastating scenario.

As hard as we try, we are unable to bargain away the event or the intense pain. We sink into depression.

Often in a family grieving the aftermath of suicide, the siblings are neglected, not deliberately, but because sometimes pain and grief consume the parents. Everyone touched by suicide grieves in their own way. Some survivors grieve quietly, masking their feelings. Others share their grief openly.

Nancy Palmer's youngest son, Geoffrey, did not feel pushed aside. Instead he spoke out and expressed his feelings to everyone who would listen.

A Day I'll Never Forget
Geoffrey Palmer

Surrounded by the cresting waves, I wade out into the ocean with mounting anticipation. Then I dive under the water. The ocean underworld has become to me a place of refuge, a place of mystery, a place of beauty, a place to lay aside painful memories. When I scuba dive, my dreams of becoming a marine biologist allow me to focus on my future.

I hope someday to discover something no one else has— like a new species of shark. When I swim with the sharks I feel like I'm a part of something wonderful. I become, in a sense, a part of the vastness of the ocean.

Usually, time in my underwater world passes too quickly, and I need to return to the surface. A small sand shark passes by gracefully. I pause. *You're not a giant, but you're a fine specimen.* I watch it glide off.

Moments later my head breaks through the surface, and I swim to shore. There I take my scuba gear off and head for my car.

Refreshed and feeling at peace, I plan my week. On the drive home I think, *Scuba diving is expensive, but I can't wait to go again, maybe Saturday. Oh, yes, this is an important week. I'm going to speak at a local high school about Jason's suicide.*

Suddenly, my mind struggles with a nagging fear that's been eating away at me. For months, Mom's been speaking with a ministry called Yellow Ribbon Suicide Prevention. She pushes herself so hard that I worry about her getting sick.

I pull into our driveway and park. When I enter the house Mom announces, "Geoffrey, the administrator at the high school you were scheduled to speak at has cancelled. He didn't want the students thinking that suicide is an option."

A wave of discouragement washes over me. Then anger surfaces. "That's stupid! Those students need to know that it's OK to ask for help."

"I know, but that's the way it is for now. We won't give up."

I nod, still feeling the weight of my disappointment, then go into my room to dress for school. I have classes to attend at Fullerton College. Sometimes I hate school. Like all young people, I can think of many other things I'd rather do. But I don't want my life to end like Jason's life. I don't want to hide away in my room and push people away. Life has its problems, but I don't want to give up. I want others to know that there are answers, and that help does exist.

Quickly, I slip into a pair of jeans and a T-shirt. On my way out I grab my baseball cap that has the black ribbon pin trimmed in gold—a pin representing my grief. A short time later, I pull into my school parking lot, park, and jump out. I head for my chemistry class to redo a lab demo I'd had trouble with.

"Geoffrey, wait up."

I stop and turn around to see who's calling me. Janet rushes to catch up, and we chat about school. Suddenly, Janet points to my cap and asks, "What's with the pin?"

"It means I'm grieving for my brother. Jason shot and killed himself last January. He was my big brother, 11 years older than me, but we had a great time together. We loved sports—played basketball together and roughhoused. I knew he fought depression, but I still can't believe he did what he did."

"Geoffrey, I'm so sorry." With an expression of shock on her face she adds, "It must be very hard on you."

"Thanks, I share my brother's story to encourage others to ask for help. Janet, if you ever know someone who talks about taking their life, take them seriously. Tell someone, so they can get help."

"Geoffrey, I will. I promise."

As Janet walks away, my thoughts flash back to the day I'll never forget—the day news reached me of my brother's suicide.

It had been a typical day with no thought of disaster looming ahead. At work a friend and I were preparing the soccer field for the kids we coached. My cell phone rang and I answered, "Hi, Mom, what's up?"

I could hardly believe what she told me.

"What happened to Jason? He did what? OK, OK, I'm on my way."

My friend saw the look of horror on my face and asked, "What's wrong?"

"I have to go home. Something's happened to Jason!"

My thoughts return to the present as I walk into my chemistry class. If I could send my brother a message, it would be, "Jason, you are missed." Always in my heart will be this question: *Jason, why did you do it?*

☆ ☆ ☆

When a rock is tossed into a lake, ripple upon ripple extends outward forming perfect circles, far beyond the center of impact. In a like manner our choices and actions have a profound effect on others around us.

The suicide of a loved one is not the end of our lives, although, at times, it feels like it. Our loved one has died, but we continue to feel like the living dead. Life has become disoriented; the future seems unreachable. It is important to focus on a goal, a vision for the future. Geoffrey learned the importance of planning and reaching past the pain—not ignoring it, but not allowing it to take away his vision.

Words from Jeenie

Seldom have I witnessed in my office a young man like Geoffrey—admitting his pain, experiencing it, yet choosing to make his life emotionally healthy and productive. Geoffrey found a place of solace in the depths of the ocean. It is imperative survivors find a place of relative peace and comfort—an oasis where their minds can be renewed and the heartache lessened for a time.

The out-of-doors is often a place of solitude and tranquility where the wounded can cry, talk with God, and express their deepest thoughts and pain. Here consolation and reassurance will begin to quiet the troubled heart.

In the next story, Karen shares how her grief brought her to a crossroad. She could either accept the finality of her son's suicide or struggle with bitterness the rest of her life—the choice was hers alone.

He Loved to Sing "Jesus Loves Me"
Karen Kosman

Our minds play tricks on us when we are grieving. There were times I felt certain I heard my son's voice. And then I'd remember our last phone conversation—the last time anyone talked with Robbie. Like a tape that had been recorded, my mind replayed our conversation over and over again.

I must have missed something in his voice, something that might have made a difference. He had called me on Thanksgiving. I'd convinced myself that Robbie was homesick and that accounted for the lack of joy in his voice. "You will be home for Christmas," I told him.

The more I'd wrestled with the question why, the deeper I sank into a pit of despair. Family and friends who tried to comfort me could not reach far enough into my prison of despair to pull me out.

At Robbie's memorial service, I sat in the church where Robbie had gone to Sunday School and thought of how he loved to sing "Jesus Loves Me." Yet, I also remembered how he'd refused to talk with others. People labeled him shy, but in my heart I felt sure it was because of his speech difficulties.

Colorful arrangements of flowers, including a beautiful bouquet of red roses, stood side-by-side at the front of the church. As I looked around this warm, familiar building, echoes of the past replayed in my mind.

Although I heard every word the minister said, I journeyed back in time....

Robbie was three, standing on our couch and looking out the sliding glass door at the rain falling. He announced, "De sky is crying."

A sob escaped my lips, and I felt my husband's hand touch mine.

Yet I moved onto another memory, Robbie's fifth birthday party in the park.

"Happy birthday, Robbie," I said, as I knelt down to kiss him. When I tried to smooth down the hairs on top of his head, that stubborn cowlick stood back up.

I smiled and asked, "Would you like to open your presents now?"

His brown eyes grew huge as he looked over the pile of presents. His expression was serious as he thought about which package to open first.

Returning to the present, I stifled a sob, and thought, *If only…* Within seconds Brother Stanley's words penetrated my heart, and I listened intently. "It's not for us to judge, but a time for us to remember God's mercy."

O God, I need You. Please help me to accept what I cannot change.

☀ ☀ ☀

Words from Jeenie

As a therapist, I often tell my clients about the concept of "old normal versus new normal." Life has been going on in a normal manner—ups and downs, little annoyances, joys—the usual stuff. Then disaster strikes and throws us smack dab in the middle of agonizing pain. During the time of mourning, we feel abnormal. Nothing makes sense; we don't care about life. Nothing brings joy. Grief has us in a vise grip, with unyielding heavy chains surrounding our hearts and minds.

I have told many clients, "If you weren't feeling abnormal during this tragedy, then I'd worry about you. This is normal for what is currently happening in your life.

"Once you have gone through this gut-wrenching painful cycle, you will establish a 'new normal.' You will again feel hope, be able to laugh, and enjoy life. The 'old normal' is gone forever, but a new one will replace it.

"A word of caution: There will always be residual pain the rest of your life. However, it will no longer control and suffocate you. Emotional health can and will be achieved, and you will be able to deal with the residual hurt."

God certainly has a purpose for us and for all the things that happen in our lives. However, we may never fully understand what those purposes are while we're on earth. It's not that God doesn't want us to know, but we are probably incapable of understanding because of our limited, finite minds.

Consider a two-year-old who sticks a fork into an electrical outlet. The parent grabs it away, yet does not try to explain to the toddler the dangers of electricity. At that age he could not grasp the concept.

Perhaps God withholds the reason trauma has occurred in our lives, not because He wants to hide something from us, but because our minds are unable to comprehend. Someday, when we see Him in His majesty and glory, we will fully understand.

REFLECTIONS

1. Bargaining: What if onlys have you said to yourself, trying to change the horrific outcome of the suicide?

2. Write down the names of two or three people with whom you can be honest and express your grief.

3. Think of several places, preferably out-of-doors, where you can find solitude and tranquility to nurture yourself. Also, find a place where you can talk honestly with God.

Prayer

Lord, my God, walk with me on this journey. Help me to set a goal for the future. Teach me to believe that I still have a purpose in life. In Jesus's name I pray, amen.

CHAPTER 3

WILL LIFE EVER SEEM NORMAL AGAIN?

My soul is weary with sorrow;
Strengthen me according to your word.
—Psalm 119:28

Karen remembers a special time when she and her husband walked on the beach after a heavy rainstorm. The sun broke through the clouds at sunset, and rays of light formed a cross upon the water. Sandpipers scurried along the seashore. The air felt crisp and smelled fresh. God's creation displayed serenity after the raging storm.

Those left behind after the suicide of a loved one often experience an emotional storm before light can shine once again on their hopelessness. They search for understanding. The weight of their grief causes a sea of uncertainty as they are tossed to and fro on their emotional waves, searching for a safe harbor.

Each family member may choose a different way to deal with grief. Even if the family grieves together in similar ways, each person will also need times of solitude. Yet all will struggle to regain a sense of normalcy. Within each soul will be a desire to find the peace God promises—a peace that surpasses all understanding.

LOOKING TO JESUS IN THE STORM

In Matthew 14:22–33, we read of a stormy sea in Galilee. Gusts of wind swirled around the small, floundering boat, while waves towered above it. The disciples were terrified when they saw Someone walking on the lake, coming toward them, and they cried out in fear.

> *But Jesus immediately said to them: "Take courage! It is I. Don't be afraid."*
> *"Lord, if it's you," Peter replied, "tell me to come to you on the water."*
> *"Come," he said.*
> —Matthew 14:27–29

Peter stepped out of the boat and walked on water. He focused his attention on Jesus with outstretched arms—arms ready to enfold him.

But at some point Peter took his eyes off Jesus and looked at the raging sea around him. That's all it took. Fear and doubt acted like an anchor, and Peter began to sink.

As waves engulfed Peter he called out, "Lord, save me," and immediately Jesus reached out His hand and grabbed hold of Peter.

For suicide survivors, the storms following their loved one's death may take many forms. For the grieving family, the stigma that accompanies suicide is an added pain for the already, hurting heart. The word *stigma* in *Merriam-Webster's 11th Collegiate Dictionary* is defined as "a mark of shame or discredit." When Karen's son died, a long-time friend commented to her, "You must feel terribly guilty." A church member told her, "I'd never commit suicide, because I don't want to go to hell."

It is important to know Scripture does not specifically address the eternal destination of a person who has taken his or her own life. There is no need to. The Bible clearly teaches that each individual's relationship to Christ determines his or her salvation, not the manner of death.

Karen felt angry and abandoned by those thoughtless comments. How could friends be so merciless? When faced with lack of understanding, the survivor tends to withdraw. The process of healing is prolonged if feelings that accompany grief are suppressed.

Survivors are already dealing with sorrow, shame, guilt, anger, and abandonment. Thoughtless comments or questions from others are inexcusable. For the survivor, it is like having a wave crash down upon them in the midst of a storm-tossed crisis. They find themselves submerged and drowning. Survivors may lose sight of friends and family that sincerely want to help.

That is why it is so important for friends and family to stay close to the grieving family over time. Often they help with funeral arrangements and prepare food. Some even help with housecleaning and other tasks. Those not able to be present phone or send cards and flowers. But at some point, all those people return to the normal routines in their own lives, leaving the survivors alone with their loss.

The emotions that surface may seem overpowering to the survivor. Yet they are part of the progression that involves all of our senses. We cannot put a time frame around those emotions. All will take place within God's timing.

As individuals, suicide survivors don't always feel the same emotions nor do they deal with their feelings in the same manner. Often individual therapy or a support group helps. Others find healing in journaling. The main point is to deal with the pain and hurt and not to stuff it!

Just as Peter called out to Jesus when doubt and fear seized him in the storm, you can take all your feelings to God and He will hold you up.

Linda, Karen Kosman's daughter, now shares how the trauma of her brother's suicide evoked other unresolved hurts from the past. Wave after wave of emotions cascaded down on her, creating confusion. Linda isolated herself from the rest of the world with an overwhelming feeling of shame. How would she ever find happiness? Would God forgive her, let alone help her?

Ashamed of the Truth
Linda Goetz

One week after my brother's memorial service, I pulled into the parking lot of the restaurant where I worked. I parked, then paused a moment beside my car, thoughts churning inside my head. *This is my first day back to work. I can't face anyone. I can't tell them how Robbie died.*

My heart seemed to skip a beat. *I don't understand why this happened—why my brother took his own life. I'll never see him again, and he'll never again share special moments in my life.* Echoing in my head over and over were the words: *Robbie hung himself.* I covered my ears, but the words would not be silenced. *God, I feel awful. I don't understand.*

As I walked through the front door of the restaurant, chattering voices and smells from the kitchen greeted me.

Sharon, my manager, stepped out of her office. "Linda, I'm sorry about your brother."

"Thank you."

"Had he been sick a long time?"

"No, it was an accident," I said trying to convince myself. "He fell off a ladder in his apartment and hit his head."

"I'm sorry," Sharon replied. "I remember how you looked forward to him coming home for Christmas."

After Sharon returned to her office I felt an overwhelming feeling of guilt, but rationalized that a lie was better then facing the shame of suicide.

Nothing settled my aching heart, not even being in a familiar environment. I kept wishing I could turn around and run. But instead, I hurried to wait on customers.

I approached a table where a man sat smiling at me. I felt my resolve slipping away, and I burst into tears. I couldn't answer this bewildered stranger who asked, "What's wrong?"

Unable to tell any of my co-workers the source of my pain, I turned and ran out of the restaurant.

I drove home, crying so hard I could hardly see. True, I felt ashamed. But behind my inability to deal with my brother's suicide, fear dominated me. Growing up, I once heard a sermon by a minister who believed people who died by suicide did not go to heaven.

I lived with shame and fear for months. As a result, I didn't move on. I didn't heal. At the time of my brother's suicide, I hadn't resolved the guilt I felt for years toward my baby sister's death due to SIDS. Then five years later, my parents divorced. All through my teen years, because of my guilt and fear, I'd acted out in various ways. Why hadn't I reached out more to the other people in my life? My life had to change.

The first step was to break up with my boyfriend of two years, a relationship that had only brought unhappiness. Next, I called home and asked, "Mom, is it OK if I move home for a while?"

"Linda, of course you can," she responded.

I began to understand no matter what you tell people, the facts don't change, and the truth remains in your heart, mind, and soul. After I moved home, Mom and I learned to communicate on a new level.

I prayed for answers. Then I remembered the words of the minister friend who presided over Robbie's memorial service. He said, "Robbie was a little boy trapped in a man's body. His clinical depression was an illness. In Matthew 19:14 Jesus said, *'Let the little children come to me, and do not hinder them, for the kingdom of heaven belongs to such as these.'* God does not punish a child having a temper tantrum. I believe Robbie has a welcome home in heaven."

I thought back to the times when my brother had been hospitalized, and we'd been told that he had a chemical imbalance. Gradually a little light began to shine on my fear and shame. I realized that no one but God is capable of judging.

Once I reached a point where I could leave what happened to my brother in God's hands, I began to accept what I could not change. I learned to cherish life more and searched my heart for new direction.

Looking back, I understand that God watched over me during those difficult years. He brought joy back into my life.

Today, I teach at a local vocational college. I've been happily married for 23 years and have two beautiful daughters.

I feel a deep compassion for people whose lives have drastically been altered by the pain of suicide. Today I am finally free of my shame. In my bedroom I have a picture of my brother and me, when we were young. I look at it and smile as I treasure the special memories of Robbie.

☀ ☀ ☀

When Robbie was four and his developmental problems became obvious, his grandmother, Betty Stokes, wrote a poem from his viewpoint.

——— ❦ ———

PLEASE!
Betty Stokes

Why don't they understand?
I try to communicate,
But I am afraid.

My years are young,
But my time is very long,
As I live within myself.

When I am spoken to, I understand,
But if I reply, I cannot make myself understood,
So I remain silent.

I'm free only in my own home,
And even then there are times when I say,
"Please help me! I feel, I love, I need—please!

———

Words from Jeenie

Death by accidents, dreaded diseases, and old age bring sympathy, Hallmark cards, and casseroles. However, with suicide, the survivors are often left with intense shame. Seldom do suicide survivors receive condolences, because people have no idea what to say. Even when they do receive encouragement, often they find it difficult to accept because they may feel undeserving or tend to blame themselves for the suicide.

Overwhelming embarrassment keeps them from being honest, even with their closest family and friends. Perhaps it is because they cannot stand to hear the comments—well meaning, but often thoughtless and glib, sometimes peppered with out-of-context Scripture. So, they suffer in silence.

What they truly need from others, though, is an expression of shared sorrow—"I'm so sorry"—accompanied by a tender hug and tears shed together.

Jeenie had the experience of losing a troubled young man when she was a high school counselor.

"You Came!"
Jeenie Gordon

Joe was an extremely emotionally troubled student, who often came to my high school office. He quietly waited until I was available. Over several years we spent many hours together as he poured out his heart. I listened.

When a week went by and I hadn't seen him, I called his home to check on him. I was told he had been admitted to a psychiatric hospital ward.

Within two weeks he was released and was again sitting outside my office. I looked into his vacant eyes. Having counseled three years in a psychiatric hospital, I immediately recognized the look of a very disturbed teenager. *Why in the world did they release him?* I thought. *It's obvious this young man needs long-term psychiatric treatment.*

"Hi, Joe. It's good to see you. I've missed you," I softly said. This time our talk was disjointed. Joe was in no shape to deal with reality nor capable of receiving encouragement. His mind was apparently in mass confusion. I felt at a loss as to how to help him.

Two days later my secretary said, "Joe's mother is on the phone and said it's urgent." Sadly, Joe had taken his life.

Tears streamed down my face as I related the news to my secretary, then headed to the principal's office. He hugged me, counseled me, and consoled me when I needed it so badly.

My mind screamed, *What could I have said to stop him? What did I do wrong? O God, why, why?*

That afternoon I drove to his parents' home, a simple abode that was clean as a whistle. It reminded me of my home growing up.

"Oh, Mrs. Gordon, You came. You came!" Over and over Joe's mother cried as I held her in my arms, our tears mingling.

A few days later, I felt the intense presence of God and His sweet Holy Spirit comforting me as I sat at the funeral mass. Even though it was in Spanish, my heart was in tune. As the casket was carried down the aisle following the service, the congregation broke out in praise songs to Jesus—a cappella. Without a doubt, I had the assurance Joe's mind was no longer clouded, and he was finally set free.

※ ※ ※

Ric Unger had been successful and self-sufficient most of his life. But after the suicide of his wife, he struggled with an emptiness he'd never experienced before. He wondered if life would ever feel normal again.

"Not One Moment More Without You, Lord"
Ric Unger

Sitting alone in our family room, I looked around. Every corner held something that reminded me of Bonnie—my precious wife of 24 years, my love, and the mother of my son. The stillness of the house closed in around me, like a black vortex that threatened to suck me in.

Bonnie's suicide created loneliness like I'd never experienced before. Imprisoned by grief, my future looked dismal. My own thoughts tormented me. *Bonnie is gone forever! All my years of hard work mean nothing anymore.*

Somehow, I realized that before I could move on I'd have to relive the painful journey Bonnie and I had made together —one inundated with bizarre mood swings that had enveloped her so quickly.

The trouble began one day when I came home from work and found my wife in a hysterical heap on the floor. Bonnie struggled with hypoglycemia and often felt depressed when her sugar levels were low. We'd been to the doctor the previous day, but I'd never seen her so out of control.

"Honey, what happened? Why are you so upset?" I asked, but my words didn't seem to reach her.

"I…I…do…don't know. Everything is sooo dark! I can't stop crying."

So once again we rushed off to our family physician, not realizing that this time Bonnie's problems were more complicated.

That night our seven-year-old son remained silent, but his eyes had a fearful, haunting look in them. At the time I didn't know what to tell him. We didn't realize it then, but our family had begun a journey into a world of manic depression.

At first, friends and family were sympathetic and offered advice. They'd make comments like: "Well, if you'd just…" Or "Just get over it!" Or "Get a part time job, if you can't work full time." On and on it went with their ideas of what would "fix the problem."

Eventually, they all stopped coming around, so Bonnie and I had to fight the battle alone.

In a manic high stage, Bonnie couldn't sleep, had tons of energy, and would go on shopping sprees. Once she called me at work and said, "Ric, I bought a mink coat today."

"Bonnie, honey, we live in sunny Southern California, and we can't afford a mink coat. We'll have to take it back."

We continued to seek help through a psychologist and a psychiatrist, who placed her on medication. Almost immediately we started seeing results and were finally working our way back to normalcy.

By staying actively involved in my wife's treatment and reading about manic depression, I learned to cope. I made a chart on her mood swings and daily monitored them.

"Ric, I'm getting better," Bonnie said one day.

"Yes, honey, I believe you are."

"I'd rather have cancer than manic depression. At least with cancer others could see the physical side of my illness."

Soon after that our hopes were crushed when Bonnie spiraled down into depression, then went through a manic high—going without sleep for five days. At the end of this time, she lost her battle and took her life.

As my painful memories faded, I fell on my knees sobbing, "I need help! God, do You hear me? I am hurting so badly! Please, help!"

Suddenly, I felt a Presence, One that brought a sense of peace.

"Is it possible? God, is it You? You are real!"

Calmness replaced my agony. Even remembering my mother's words, "There is no God," did not threaten my new sense of truth. All through my childhood and into my adolescence I heard those words. Yet, the very God who I'd been told did not exist had just drawn me to Him!

From that moment on, I continued to grieve—but not alone. I started going to church and accepted Jesus Christ as my personal Savior.

Sixteen years have passed since my wife's suicide. Today, my son is married, and I've been blessed with a granddaughter.

I'm happily remarried and joyful in the knowledge that my strength comes from Jesus. God helped me to reclaim normalcy in life.

A growing desire to help others fight depression grew inside of me. I prayed for direction. At a men's Christian conference, one of the speakers asked, "What are you going to do with the rest of your life?" I knew then God wanted me to start a ministry, an outreach designed to help those who are struggling with depression or have a family member who is mentally ill. Today that vision is a reality in a ministry at Saddleback Church in Southern California called Bring Back the Hope. Many lives are being touched, and I am grateful to be a part of God's plan to bring hope and understanding to others.

(Ric succumbed to cancer in 2007, but the ministry he started at Saddleback Church continues today.)

☀ ☀ ☀

Words from Jeenie

Over the years, I've had numerous bipolar patients (manic-depressive). These patients have a chemical imbalance in their brains, and, in my professional opinion, lifelong medication is needed to alleviate the extreme highs and lows.

I've often asked a client, "So, when did you go off your medication?" It is especially noticeable when the client enters into the manic phase. This phase usually feels good. They're on top of the world and enjoy the euphoria. However, they will soon plummet into deep depression. Often that is the state in which suicide occurs.

Some clients complain about the side effects of medication, such as grogginess or weight gain. Others start feeling better so they convince themselves they can stop taking their medicine.

Being a type 2 diabetic (adult onset), I explain to clients how I must take medication for the rest of my life. If I don't, eventually I'll die—or lose my eyesight or a limb. I can usually feel good without the medication, but my body is being irreparably damaged.

Thus, after the diagnosis, the bipolar patient must take medication throughout his life. Unfortunately, many do not, and it is next to impossible for a spouse to control the taking of medication. When I counseled at a psychiatric hospital, patients held the pills in their cheeks. Then they spit them out at the first opportunity.

In the next story, life for the Zingaro family seemed to be all they wanted it to be. Their eldest son, Alex, a junior in college, lived in his own apartment. Although they didn't see Alex as often as they'd liked, he called home on a regular basis. Bret, their youngest son, kept his parents active with his high school sports. Then with no warning, a phone call came, shattering their contentment.

When the Unexpected Happens
Patti Zingaro

The sound of pounding and scraping came from our kitchen where a contractor worked. The phone rang, and I raced to answer it, "Hello."

"Patti, this is Scott, I'm sorry to call you like this, but I'm worried about Alex."

"Really, why?"

"I haven't seen him in a day and a half."

"You mean he hasn't called or left you a note?"

"Right."

Alex always communicated with his roommate Scott out of common courtesy. I felt fear's cold fingers run down my spine. My mind screamed, *Alex is OK. He has to be! He just started college and a new job. Where would he go?*

I began making calls and checking with all his friends. A trip to Alex's apartment revealed that all his belongings were still there. It seemed as if Alex had vanished.

Our panic mounted, and we called the police. An extensive search began. We contacted the media and had a television interview in our home. Still no Alex. We prayed daily and hoped. As time passed we began to fear that Alex had run into some kind of foul play. Not knowing caused sleepless nights and days without being able to eat. We passed out flyers and waited.

Then another of Scott's friends called, "Patti, we found a note in a document on Alex's computer."

Mom, Dad, and Bret,

By now you're probably wondering what happened to me. I just had to get away. I don't know what's taken over me. I'm not happy with my life anymore. I don't know where I am going, but I am going to get on the road and go. This is nobody's fault but my own. I love you more than you'll ever know, and I love my friends. I'll see you soon.

Love,

Alex

We were all relieved. After all, Alex had said, "I'll see you soon." At least we knew something.

The police called off the search for Alex because they said he went off on his own. The media called and asked, "Why did we lie?"

Thoroughly exhausted, we decided the best thing to do was to go on with our lives. We had no idea when Alex would return—maybe he'd gone to Colorado or Canada. He loved to snowboard. I pushed away the nagging whisper in my heart that said none of this made sense.

Seven days after Alex went missing, we received a phone call. I prayed it would be Alex.

"Hello."

"Mrs. Zingaro, this is the San Bernardino police. Is there anyone there with you?"

"Yes, my husband, Al. I'll get him." *Oh no!* my mind agonized, *It's about Alex. Something has happened to Alex!*

"Al, come quickly! It's a phone call from the police. I think something has happened to Alex." I picked up the phone once again, my heart racing. I knew the news would not be good, but no one could ever be prepared to hear, "We are sorry to tell you that some hikers in Big Bear found Alex dead. He hung himself."

After the shocking news of Alex's death reached his friends, we began receiving phone calls. Some friends shared that Alex told them, "I am somewhat depressed." But he always attached it to something like, "I don't have a special girl," or "I'm having trouble finding a job," so it didn't seem like anything serious. None of the pieces of the puzzle fit together.

Sometimes I've wondered if we didn't see Alex's depression because he was living away from home. But Alex had close friends, and none of them saw it coming. We had no idea that Alex was suffering. We don't even know when his depression began. Alex apparently thought he could handle it.

When we returned to Alex's apartment, we discovered a large supply of Saint-John's-wort. He had apparently tried self-medication using this herbal remedy for depression. Alex had no history of serious problems, no social issues, and no problems in school. He always had lots of friends. He was athletic and handsome. He loved life.

I think what happened is his depression hit so fast it simply got away from him. Then when it grew bigger than life, he tried unsuccessfully to run from it.

(Today Patti has moved to Colorado. She is involved in a ministry called Second Wind Fund Counseling that raises money for kids who need counseling, and she continues to keep in touch with Nancy Palmer and Terri Evans.)

☀ ☀ ☀

Words from Jeenie

As a therapist, I often see that men tend to hide their depression. In their thinking, it's unmanly to complain—especially about depression. They believe they can handle it, and it will soon pass.

Males usually think things through while women generally talk things through. Therefore, cocooning is usually not a healthy move for a man. The spiral of depression is more likely to take them quickly into the depths of despair. Rather than calling a family member, they suffer in silence.

In their depressed, clouded judgment, they think the only solution to the problem is to end the pain. They don't stop to realize it is a quick and permanent solution.

"If there are a thousand steps between us and God, He will take all but one. He will leave the final one for us. The choice is ours."
—Max Lucado

Reflections

1. Are you struggling with guilt? Write those feelings out. Take them to the Lord in prayer.

2. Are you struggling with shame? Write out your feelings regarding that too.

3. Then create a mental picture of a light switch and turn it on. Let the light flood the room. Let God's light push away your shame.

Prayer

Lord, I call upon You to fill me with Your love. I need Your comfort daily. No longer can I travel through life without You. Strengthen me with Your peace that surpasses all understanding. In Jesus's name I pray, amen.

CHAPTER 4

THIS TOO
WILL PASS

May the Lord answer you when you are in distress;
may the name of the God of Jacob protect you.
—Psalm 20:1

September 11, 2001, is a day that will never be forgotten. Forever seared in the minds of Americans is the image of two commercial airliners, with innocent people onboard, smashing into New York's World Trade Center. Clouds of smoke rose high in the sky as fire devoured the towers. They collapsed and came crashing to the ground. Sirens wailed as people panicked and ran for cover.

Yet, amongst the rubble that had once been the Twin Towers, two metal supports were found. They had been welded together by the intense heat that engulfed the towers, their purpose forever changed, their shapes forever altered. Now they formed a perfect cross. Today that cross stands at the memorial site known as Ground Zero.

In a similar manner, the tragedy of suicide leaves our lives in rubble. After we have spent years building a relationship, suddenly that person is gone. We are left with unfulfilled dreams. Somehow suicide survivors, as well as those who have contemplated or attempted suicide, must crawl out from beneath the wreckage of sorrow to rebuild their broken lives.

Strewn across the once solid foundation of life is emotional debris. Sorrow and guilt have crashed into their hearts and remain buried there. Life constantly changes in a perpetual cycle that normally brings growth. Yet, in these circumstances, we ask, "Is sorrow a necessary part of this cycle, and will it soon pass away?" Our sorrow has brought us to ground zero. Yet the promise fulfilled by Jesus on the Cross is that this too shall pass away. Through His love, we will one day begin to heal and move forward.

In Max Lucado's book *No Wonder They Call Him the Savior* he writes:

> What do you do when words won't come? When all the nouns and verbs lay deflated at your feet, with what do you communicate? When even the loftiest statements stumble, what do you do? Are you one of the fortunate who isn't ashamed to let a tear take over? Can you be so happy that your eyes water and your throat swells? Can you be so proud that your pupils blur and your vision mists? And in sorrow, do you let your tears decompress that tight chest and untie that knot in your throat?

Belinda understands the cleansing power behind tears. She is a suicide survivor who has walked through the night of grief and has resurfaced into the sunlight. Today she reaches out to help others by sharing her journey.

He Ain't Heavy
Belinda Howard Smith

I'm called a survivor—one of many left behind in the wake of a suicide. At age 52, my older brother took his life. You may have heard the statement: "Men use guns. It's fast and final." To some Ricky is just another statistic proving the point: He suffered from a bipolar disorder and had a traumatic brain injury caused by an accident just a couple of years before he took his life with a shotgun one October.

Yet to family and friends, Ricky will always be more than a statistic. At his funeral I hoped Ricky watched from heaven. With the church packed with friends and family, Ricky would have witnessed how many lives he'd touched. He had more ex-in-laws filling rows than actual family members. Though divorced after 26 years of marriage, his former wife, who remained his best friend, had difficulty comforting their two teenage children. There were more survivors—an 82-year-old mother, five siblings, their spouses, and their children—who mourned his death.

My brother, Ricky, had been a loving husband, father, and successful businessman. Then a mental illness destroyed a 26-year marriage and eventually his life. His first "episode" struck at age 46, and later an accident resulted in a traumatic brain injury. Life just kept pulling him down.

Then Ricky made a fatal decision. He stopped taking his medication, and depression once again overwhelmed him. I feared he would take his life. He lived 500 miles away, and I called him almost every day. He didn't know that I could hear his muffled whimpering as he held back his tears.

Every time I talked to him, I told him that I loved him. I told him that his family needed him. I offered to buy back his beloved dogs that he had recently sold. I hoped the dogs would give him something to care for—a reason to get out of bed in the morning. I prayed, and I asked others to pray—but none of those efforts was enough.

Then the dreaded day arrived. My brother called and said, "Ricky shot himself."

O God, I thought, *this news is too painful to bear, and what about Mom? She lost her husband 2 years ago after 59 years of marriage. How is she going to handle the loss of her son, too?*

He'd been found slumped in his chair—a blood-soaked Bible open at his feet, turned to Romans 8:38–39, which says:

For I am convinced that neither death nor life, neither angels nor demons, neither the present nor the future, nor any powers, neither height nor depth, nor anything else in all creation, will be able to separate us from the love of God that is in Christ Jesus our Lord.

I questioned God, *How much more can I handle?* At the time news reached me about my brother, my own daughter recently had been placed in a psychiatric hospital and diagnosed with bipolar.

Just a week earlier in a phone conversation with Ricky, I told him about his niece. He'd cried—this time not holding back his tears. Now I needed to tell my daughter about her uncle Ricky. Where would she find hope in the midst of her own illness?

Within those first few hours after hearing the news, my mind whirled with conflicting thoughts and emotions. Oddly enough, I felt relief. I no longer had to fear that Ricky would take his life. I could quit worrying. I could quit praying about it. I could quit thinking about what I could do to help him.

I thought, *I am entitled not to feel guilty.* After all, I did everything I could for him. Many times I told him, "I love you." I offered help. I prayed. I did everything I knew to do.

But guilt and remorse moved in anyway. Consuming thoughts of: *If only I would have, if I could have, if I had only known… then maybe he would still be here.*

In my mind, I replayed what must have been his last moments. I pictured him going through the motions of getting his shotgun. I pictured him silently whimpering as he held back his tears. I don't believe he wanted to die. I believe he thought he was doing his family a favor.

It has been four years since Ricky's death. I miss him. I think of him every day. I no longer replay what might have been his last moments. I picture him smiling, looking like he did in happier times. I can hear his chuckle, and often I feel like he is assuring me that all is well. I remind my daughter to remember him that way—the "real" uncle Ricky.

If he could see me now, he would see my tears dripping on the keyboard—my pauses to stop and sob. He would see how much I still hurt. I can almost hear him say, "Don't cry. It won't be that long before I'll see you again."

And I cry every time I hear the song, "He Ain't Heavy, He's My Brother." I would have carried him for a lifetime.

֍ ֍ ֍

Words from Jeenie

Families often deal with a depressed member for years, which takes an enormous toll. Fear and anxiety become a familiar part of life. As grief recovery ensues, and reality begins to take effect, people eventually realize there was nothing more they could have done. They cannot force a person to seek medical help or take medication. They cannot prevent suicide.

Let me share with you the following story about a pastor.

He was a respected leader in his denomination—a wise and godly man. Young men sought his counsel when they believed God had called them into ministry. "What are the pitfalls? How will I know for certain God has put His hand on my life? Where will I go for training?" were some of the questions he fielded. Beginning pastors asked his advice, as did seasoned men of God.

Yet, something went wrong. He became deeply depressed and lived in a black hole from which he could find no exit. Not willing to seek medical help, he and his wife struggled for years. His wife did not want to interfere by seeking help or even mentioning it to their family and closest friends. They both suffered in silence.

One cloudy day, he drove onto a long expansion bridge over a Pacific Ocean harbor, stopped his car in the middle, stepped out, and jumped.

Many pastors in his denomination believed suicide meant eternal damnation, but at his funeral, they began to realize this was an act of a godly man who, in a moment of insanity, made an instant and final decision.

His dear wife breathed a sigh of relief because the days of deep emotional pain had ended. Yet, guilt haunted her.

I've explained to grieving clients that guilt almost always follows death, whether suicide or natural death. We have the irrational sense that somehow we could have prevented the death—that we didn't do enough. The "what ifs" and "if onlys" become our nagging companions. Emotional health comes when, in time, we are able to accept God's gift of relief—without guilt.

Psalm for the Troubled Heart
Charles R. Brown

There is no cloud that blocks Your view,
O God, of all beneath its black canopy.
There is no night so dark that You cannot see.
There are no waves high enough
to wash away Your everlasting purpose.
There is no forest thick enough
that prohibits You from finding the lost.
There is no illness toxic enough
to rob the soul of life in You.
There is no loss great enough
to bankrupt the child of God.
There is no ocean deep enough
to swallow the sound of Your voice.

There is no scholar smart enough
to figure You out.
There are no surprises
beyond Your understanding.
There are no prodigals
that You would not seek to embrace.
There is no distress, no trouble,
that baffles You.
There is no provision better
than that which comes from Your hand.
There is no greater gift
than the One You have given.

———

Jeanne didn't know the young mother of four who had recently died, but whispers circulated quickly through the small, Christian school her children attended.

The Heart's Last Cry
Jeanne Pallos

Mystery and secrecy surrounded the mother's death, and I noticed the teachers and school principal, when asked about the incident, always gave the same vague answer: "She fell in the shower and hit her head." However, the story seemed to vary a little with each person telling it, and they always avoided eye contact and turned away.

"It's tragic that four children are left without a mother," was the consensus of opinion. Yet no one seemed willing to talk about the incident.

What are they hiding? I wondered.

Over the years I had gotten to know the principal and felt I could approach him for an honest answer. "Mr. Graves, what happened to that mother? Did she really die in a fall?"

"No," he said, "she didn't fall in the shower. She took her own life, but the family doesn't want anyone to know."

My heart sank. Why would a mother of four children take her own life? Why would she inflict this dark legacy upon her children's hearts for a lifetime? Had her family fabricated the story about her death to protect her children? Why couldn't the Christian community talk honestly about her death?

Months later, another mother I carpooled with mentioned the incident. "Did you know her?" she asked.

"No," I answered, "but it's tragic."

"Did you know that she committed suicide?"

I noted a hint of disgust in her voice. "Yes," I replied.

"Well," she went on, "that was the most selfish thing that mother could do. Suicide is the ultimate act of selfishness."

The woman's words stung me—*selfish*? How could this woman pass judgment?

Many years later, as a Christian, I also wrestled with depression and thoughts of suicide. I tried to talk with trusted spiritual leaders and friends.

"Just get your eyes off yourself," someone said.

"You need to praise more," another person advised and handed me a how-to book on Christian praising. These comments caused me to force a smile and push my feelings of despair deeper into my heart. Like the young mother who took her life, I longed to be free from my emotional pain. I thought if I practiced the spiritual disciplines more and had more faith, the depression would lift.

It did not. I sank into hopelessness because I felt like a failure as a Christian. *Christians don't get depressed. Christians don't think about suicide.*

One night, I screamed out to God on my knees, as a giant invisible force urged me to take my own life. "Just do it," the voice kept saying. I struggled the whole night between the forces of life and death.

Early the next morning I called a counselor, and within hours I received professional help. After a couple of sessions and tests my doctor said, "It's biochemical." Within weeks, counseling and proper medication balanced my brain chemistry and lifted the cloud of depression that almost claimed my life.

I thought of the young mother who had taken her own life. Was it a final act of selfishness? No, I believe it was more like a final act of desperation—the same kind of despair I had wrestled with and conquered by God's grace and with professional help.

Maybe that mother's life could have been saved if her feelings of suicide could have been openly shared. Maybe if she felt comfortable telling the Christian community about her depression, she could have received help.

Suicide—the despairing heart's final cry. If you know someone who is suicidal, listen and believe. Then guide them to safe, supportive counselors who are trained to listen and to help them.

≫⸝⸜ ≫⸝⸜ ≫⸝⸜

Words from Jeenie

Almost daily, I look into the vacant, pain-filled eyes of a depressed client. Suicidal thoughts are often whispered. As I carefully check to see if the person has a suicidal plan, he or she often informs me of how society often disdains or dismisses depression and suicidal ideation—in ways similar to the comments Jeanne heard. Sometimes it's a deterrent. Sometimes it isn't.

No other death is treated in such a cruel manner by society. Condolences come when disease takes a person's life. Don't the survivors of death by suicide require just as much, if not more, concern and compassion from others?

For the grief-stricken relative, healing is a long and arduous journey. However, let's remember Jesus is the Great Healer.

A Desperate Woman Reaches Out for Jesus

No one paid any attention to the woman as she pushed her way through the crowd. The woman had struggled with an illness for 12 years. She'd seen doctors and had exhausted all her funds, but her condition grew worse. No one was able to find a solution to her constant bleeding. Exhaustion claimed every moment of her day. She had no answers, no hope, and no secure future. She felt physically and emotionally exhausted.

Then she heard about the Teacher, the One who healed the blind, the lepers, the lame. Perhaps He could heal her, too. Yes, if He could, the insistent bleeding would stop. A new determination surged through her entire being as slowly she pushed her way through the crowd.

Just a few more steps, she thought. *If I just touch his cloak, I'm sure I'll be healed.*

She came up behind him and touched the edge of his cloak, and immediately her bleeding stopped.

"Who touched me?" Jesus asked.

When they all denied it, Peter said, "Master, the people are crowding and pressing against you."

But Jesus said, "Someone touched me; I know that power has gone out from me."

Then the woman, seeing that she could not go unnoticed, came trembling and fell at his feet. In the presence of all the people, she told why she had touched him and how she had been instantly healed. Then he said to her, "Daughter, your faith has healed you. Go in peace."

—Luke 8:44–48

The woman's name is not mentioned, but that's not important. Jesus called her "daughter." He understood how much she'd suffered and knew to whom she belonged. He offered healing and peace after a long struggle.

In the following story, a mother grieves the recent loss of her daughter. Through tears she stores up a treasure of hope for a future where joy will return.

Jolene's Treasures
Darlene Franklin

Two or three days before her 24th birthday, my daughter Jolene took her own life. The days following the discovery of her body ran together in a blur. I talked on the phone until my voice grew hoarse. Family drove in from out of state, and we planned and held a memorial service.

Once everyone had gone home, my mother and I were left alone with our grief. For a number of nights, we stared at a square, lilac-colored metal box that held Jolene's treasures.

"It's time," my mother said one evening after dinner. So I broke open the lock. *What had Jolene treasured enough to keep in a special place?* I wondered.

The item on top was a small bag of polished stones from the Holy Land. Looking inside, I realized Jolene had added a few other unique rocks. She always noticed unusual objects of various colors and shapes on the ground, and she loved to collect stones, twigs, branches, and leaves—anything that caught her interest. Her brother, Jaran, mentioned her love of nature in what he wrote for her memorial service.

Tears filled my eyes as I ran my fingers over a small box that held pins from the 2002 Olympics. I thought back fondly to the time when Jolene and I had taken part in a missions outreach in Salt Lake City. She excelled in pin trading and delighted in her final collection. Each pin represented a different event—skating, skiing, hockey, etc.

I thought back to that special vacation where we spent our mornings ministering to the security staff at the ski jump venue. During their breaks, they huddled in a tent only slightly warmer than the frigid outside air. We served hot cocoa and sat down to talk with them. One worker told Jolene, "You're a deep thinker." Jolene loved the opportunity to share her faith.

Next I held up a turquoise bracelet and thought back to another vacation that began with a 12-hour bus trip to Santa Fe, New Mexico. My memories of that experience are as golden as the summer sun. We ate sweet potato fries, went to a free concert, and later shopped at the town square.

I could still picture the American Indians, sitting around the town square with their jewelry, displayed for sale on colorful blankets. That's where Jolene bought her turquoise bracelet. On the way home, the driver stopped the bus so we could cross the bridge spanning the Rio Grande on foot.

Next to the bracelet was a little glass tube, a pipette of fool's gold we bought while traveling through Colorado's Rocky Mountains. In a whirlwind weekend with Jaran, we went from Buena Vista to Vail, stopping at all the scenic points in between. Jolene had a hard time that weekend. She had recently changed medications for the mental illness that plagued her, borderline personality disorder, and they hadn't yet taken effect. Still, we piled memory upon memory. Jolene loved finding the fool's gold. Looking at these mementos made me realize how much these family trips meant to Jolene— although she never told me with words.

Below a cotton pad, I found dozens of coins from all over the world. Jolene collected American coins from the year of her birth, 1984, as well as older coins (from the 1930s and 1940s). She had lots of coins from Canada and Mexico, but the number of coins from around the world astonished me. There were coins with Chinese characters; coins from Bermuda, Chile, and Panama; and also European coins from Poland, Holland, and Italy, as well as from a former Soviet country that we could not identify.

At the very bottom of the treasure box lay a picture of Jolene with her fingerprints on the reverse side, her own form of identification, as well as her Social Security card, Colorado ID, and birth certificate.

Looking at her treasures brought home my loss in a new way. I have lost someone unique and special, someone who treasured God's earth and the people on it. I sobbed from a broken heart.

A friend said, "Jolene's treasures now include your tears, little pearls of wisdom and love." They are my riches sowed in the soil of my grief, so that as Psalm 126:5 promises, *"Those who sow in tears will reap with songs of joy."*

☀ ☀ ☀

Words from Jeenie

People grieve differently. There is no right or wrong way, only what comforts and fits the personality of the mourner.

Having lost my mother to cancer decades ago, I was unable to look at her photo or keepsakes for several years. And many years passed before I was able to visit her grave.

Jolene's mother, however, was greatly comforted by her daughter's treasures. Each time she gently held them, a bit of pain was eased. In the ensuing years, these collections will be a constant and precious reminder of Jolene, who lived her life to the fullest and continues to do so with the Lord.

God's Word provided comfort for Terri Evans when she called out for His help. That lifeline is there for you, too.

Don't Be Quiet!
Terri Evans

Sitting alone in my kitchen, I glanced up at a picture of Jesus with a teenage boy kneeling before Him. The young man's head rested in Jesus's lap, and on the ground beside him lay a pair of handcuffs. A neighbor had given the picture to me after my son Sean's funeral.

Tears filled my eyes. *Why are You silent, Lord? I don't feel like Terri anymore. When I look at my reflection in the mirror, a thin stranger looks back. My stomach burns and is constantly tied in a knot.*

After Sean's funeral, I struggled with strong emotions of abandonment and anger. Yet, I did my best to push those emotions away. I needed release from the ongoing agony. Otherwise I'd never be able to heal. At the time of Sean's suicide, my eldest son was 20 and very independent. I had expected to be mothering Sean for many more years. After his death I lost my identity.

It helped knowing that friends were praying daily for our family. How could I tell anyone how much I hurt? I prayed and pleaded, "God, all my life I've been a Christian. I feel lost. Why can't I feel Your presence?"

I made some tea, hoping that the warmth would help my stomach. I thought about my morning at work. *Even there, in familiar surroundings, I can hardly function.*

I walked down the hall to Sean's room and collapsed to the floor—broken and vulnerable. In my heart, God reminded me of these words to touch and comfort me.

"I have told you these things, so that in me you may have peace. In this world you will have trouble. But take heart! I have overcome the world."
—John 16:33

Hot tears began to stream down my cheeks, as other verses in the Book of John came to me.

"Do not let your hearts be troubled. Trust in God; trust also in me. In my Father's house are many rooms; if it were not so, I would have told you. I am going there to prepare a place for you."
—John 14:1–2

As I thought of those words, I felt a renewed sense of peace. I envisioned God on His throne. Mentally I placed my anguish at His feet.

"Lord," I prayed, "show me what I need to do."

Eventually, the answer came. God wanted me to reach out to other families who had children who were bipolar. I had to do whatever possible to stop suicide from claiming more victims. I realized that by letting God use my pain, my loss of Sean could become a lifeline to other adolescents. This would spare the tears and broken hearts of other mothers.

In my moment of truth, I realized that God had never left me, nor had He been silent. In His time He sent me His grace.

☀ ☀ ☀

Praise be to the God and Father of our Lord Jesus Christ, the Father of compassion and the God of all comfort, who comforts us in all our troubles, so that we can comfort those in any trouble with the comfort we ourselves have received from God.
—2 Corinthians 1:3–4

After we have emerged from enormous pain and have experienced God's comfort, we will be used by God to comfort and counsel others in the ensuing years. Our pain will not be in vain.

Words from Jeenie

Dear friends of mine lost their 12-year-old son to cancer. Now some years later, in Brazil, they have an amazing ministry of comfort to parents who are also experiencing the same trauma. They built a home to house parents while their children are going through cancer treatments. Not only do the parents and children receive tender loving care, but also the gospel of Christ.

REFLECTIONS

1. What special memory of your loved one is a treasure in your heart?

2. What feelings accompany those memories?

3. If the memories bring tears, let them fall. If they bring laughter, know that is good for our spirits.

Prayer

Lord, help me to feel Your comfort in my grief. Sometimes as my tears fall, I feel like the tears of angels mingle with mine. I cling to Your promise that joy will return. I thank You for the sweet memories. Bring me quickly, Lord, to the other side of my grief— a time You have promised when I can bring comfort to others. In Jesus's name I pray, amen.

CHAPTER 5

LEARNING TO LET GO

"He will wipe every tear from their eyes. There will be no more death or mourning or crying or pain, for the old order of things has passed away."
—Revelation 21:4

L earning to let go after a tragedy is something people have struggled with since Adam and Eve. Bitterness, anger, and guilt are strong emotions that can keep our souls in bondage. Yet we can learn lessons from those who have suffered great loss, trusted God, and used His Word as a bridge to renewal. In Corrie ten Boom's *The Hiding Place* we find such an example.

LESSONS FROM A CONCENTRATION CAMP
Released from the Ravensbrück concentration camp in Nazi Germany in 1944, Corrie ten Boom refused to be filled with bitterness. Soon after, at the age of 52, she stepped out in faith and became an evangelist.

She wanted to fulfill her sister Betsie's dying words in the camp: "[We] must tell people what we have learned here. We must tell them that there is no pit so deep that He is not deeper still. They will listen to us, Corrie, because we have been here."

Corrie, with her silver hair, rosy cheeks, and sparkling eyes captivated audiences as she traveled to more than 60 countries, telling of God's love and forgiveness. When she spoke she told people that God's truth still shines even in the deepest darkness and that His comfort is ever present.

After she spoke at a church in Munich, Germany, a man she recognized approached her—a former SS man from Ravensbrück. He thrust his hand out to shake hers. "How grateful I am for your message, *Fraulein*," he said, "to think that, as you say, He has washed my sins away!"

At first Corrie kept her hand by her side. She prayed that Jesus would give her the ability to forgive this man. In her own words:

> As I took his hand the most incredible thing happened. From my shoulder along my arm and through my hand a current seemed to pass through me to him, while into my heart sprang a love for this stranger that almost overwhelmed me.
>
> And so I discovered that it is not on our forgiveness any more than on our goodness that the world's healing hinges, but on His.
>
> —*The Hiding Place*

The anger and bitterness for some suicide survivors may seem like the pit Betsie described. And although it's a pit we have to climb out of, God supplies the ladder and gives us the strength we need. If we think of each day as an opportunity to climb one more rung, then the top of the pit no longer seems out of reach. If you see yourself in this situation, ask others to pray for you. Then with God's help you can find the courage to start climbing the ladder.

Like Corrie, every survivor needs to seek some measure of closure. For many it means the ability to return to jobs, school, caring for families, and helping other family members return to their daily routines. One day at a time, we step forward, understanding that this is made possible through God's strength—not ours.

King David expresses his feelings on this in Psalm 40:2. "*He lifted me out of the slimy pit, out of the mud and mire; he set my feet on a rock and gave me a firm place to stand.*"

Words from Jeenie

Many times while speaking on forgiveness, I have used the illustration of Corrie ten Boom. After visiting the German prison camp Dachau, and later Auschwitz, I could easily visualize the circumstances of Corrie's imprisonment.

Then later I was blessed with the opportunity to visit Corrie. I stood at her bedside where she sat writing yet another book.

"Jeenie, sit on my bed," she invited. A woman in her 80s, Corrie had the peace of Jesus etched across her face. She radiated contentment and forgiveness.

Forgiveness is not for the benefit of the other person—it's for our benefit. God knows the freedom that forgiveness will bring to our broken, troubled hearts. Even though we will be able to recite the facts of the trauma we encountered, they will no longer have a stranglehold on our emotions.

The road to forgiveness is long and generally cannot be traveled until after the first few years of grieving. There will come a time when God whispers into our hearts, *It's time to begin the journey.*

Karen shares a time, two years after the loss of her son, when she found her grief once more resurfacing. Karen thought she had moved on, and she tried to push the feelings away. She quickly learned, though, that there are consequences, emotionally and physically, when we refuse to let the tears fall.

A Condo on the Beach
Karen Kosman

Finding the courage to face the many facets of suicide takes time. There is no set time schedule. For me it became a day-to-day struggle. My work, my friends, and my family helped to ease the pain. I poured myself into my profession as a training coordinator for new phlebotomists. I loved to spend time with patients, encouraging them and training new employees. I began to smile again and function within a normal routine.

Then one day at the hospital, I went with a new phlebotomist to assist her. A guard sat outside one patient's room, but I had no idea why. I went to the nurses station to inquire and learned a teenage boy had attempted suicide, and his parents hired the guard to watch him.

As we entered the room, a pale, sad teen looked up. He said, "It won't do any good, you know?"

"Tell me," I asked, "what won't do any good?"

"The guard. I'll go home sooner or later."

"Is your life that painful?" I asked.

"Who cares?"

"I do."

His eyes softened.

As I left his room, I determined that I'd visit him later, but that opportunity never arrived. The next day he was moved to another facility. The incident with this suicidal young man once again dredged up the feelings surrounding my own son's death.

I began dreaming about Robbie. In one dream, cliffs stood high above the beach where houses overlooked the ocean. Beautiful pine trees surrounded the houses, and a wooden staircase led down to the shore. Below on the beach I sat on a log. In the distance my son approached. I called to him, "Robbie, I want to tell you something."

Instantly he vanished.

A few weeks later I shared my reoccurring dream with a close friend. Cynthia was an author and inspirational speaker who dealt with human emotions all the time in her ministry. I knew she would understand.

"Karen, I believe this is part of your grieving process. Tomorrow is your day off. Why don't you call a Christian counselor? Therapy can help you deal with your feelings."

Cynthia thought for a moment before continuing, "I have a condo in Oregon. Why don't you and John spend your vacation there this year?"

"We'd love to, Cynthia, and I'll think about the counseling."

The next morning I made the call to begin my counseling. In therapy I found permission to express my fears, anger, and doubts. I also told of my hopes for the future. My counselor suggested I keep a journal.

Between therapy sessions, I journaled. Then I wrote about my dream, only I changed the outcome: *I sat on a log and watched Robbie approach, but this time he sat down next to me. I looked into his eyes and said, "I miss you. I felt angry at you for leaving the way you did. I even felt angry that God hadn't stopped you. I didn't understand the depth of your pain, and that made me angry at myself."*

As I wrote those words, I felt the anger being lifted. Tears fell as I continued to write. *Goodbye, son. I love you. I'm not angry anymore.*

But in my writing, unlike my dream, Robbie stood up and smiled. Then he walked back down the beach. He stopped and turned to wave. I waved back and felt the freedom to let go.

During my next session, I shared my story with my counselor. A few days later, over lunch, Cynthia read my journal. She smiled and said, "I think you'll find that beach when you visit Oregon."

I didn't understand what she meant until John and I arrived at Cynthia's vacation home. The condo was surrounded by pine trees and sat on a cliff, overlooking the ocean. We climbed down a wooden staircase to the beach below.

"Lord," I prayed, "this is the beach in my dream—but I've never been here before!"

A gentle breeze touched my face, and I relaxed as the waves lapped onto the shore. I realized that God knows all things. He knows my coming and my going, my thoughts and my dreams. He sent me my dreams to help me to let go.

☀ ☀ ☀

Two years seems to be a typical time of intense sorrow and numbness for those who have lost a loved one. Over and over, I have seen the time frame played out with students and clients in therapy.

It takes about two years before the force of reality hits home. Truth knocks the mourner down with a blow similar to a heavyweight boxer hitting him in the gut. The person understands the great loss will last the rest of his life, and he hates it. Often I hear the expression, "I despise my life, and I can't stand the pain. It's eating me up inside."

Family and friends, who gathered close for the first few months or a year, eventually go on with their lives. Rarely do they give the mourner's loss another conscious thought. For the most part, there is no longer a human source in which to find comfort, thus, loneliness and isolation can become overwhelming.

Journaling is a valid, healthy way to start to resolve the issues. Talking things over with God, as Karen did, helps the grief-stricken person to slowly begin to move on with life.

I've made it a practice for many years to have a daily prayer list for those who are grieving the loss of their loved one. At the end of the year, I write them a note. Generally I begin: *Rarely have I missed a day praying for you and your family during your first year of mourning…* I have received numerous return notes telling me how my prayers have impacted and comforted their lives. One mother at my high school wrote: *If my daughter would have had you as her counselor, she would still be alive today.*

We have a responsibility and obligation to continue to support those who mourn. Romans 12:15 states, "*Weep with them that weep*" (KJV).

To Our Sister
Gary Sumner

We hate that thing you did.
It did not solve one thing.
We doubt you thought it through.
How could you plan such pain?

Your life was not just yours—
A part of it was ours.
The ones you left behind
Cruel emptiness now know.

We'd plans and hopes and dreams
Of times with you, dear one.
Events need not be grand—
Your presence was enough.

A future filled with joy
And days of happiness,
With loved ones all around
Were always wished for you.

Now do you hear the tears,
That come to us unbidden?
We ache to think of such
A future swept away.

Maybe you have seen the painting of Jesus standing at a door knocking. Of course, that closed door represents the human heart. Is there something locked away in your heart— something unsaid, something undone, something that needs completion? In the next story Kristin opened the door so God could bring closure many years after her dad's death.

Finding Closure
Kristin Lee Taylor

"Sarah committed suicide. We are having the funeral service at a church near your house. I hope you can come."

The voice on the answering machine sounded mechanical, void of feeling. My heart went out to my husband's sister, Ann. I could not even imagine what she was going through.

Although Ann's daughter, Sarah, lived half an hour from our home, we hadn't seen her since our wedding nine years before. She was pregnant at the time, and I suddenly realized she was leaving a 9-year-old daughter behind. We had tried to get together with her and her husband, Hiro, but they never seemed available.

When I asked Ann how her daughter had died, she replied, "I don't know. I don't want to know!" Ann's family were committed Christians, but their adopted daughter, Sarah, who was Korean, had adamantly stated, "I have no use for the white man's God."

I thought of her words as I stood over the open casket, staring at the body of the 30-year-old woman. She looked so young. I saw cuts on the edges of her wrists; her hands were folded in front of her. I drew the conclusion that she must have slit her wrists on that fateful Saturday night, but none of us will ever know for sure....

After the funeral, Ann said, "We are leaving tomorrow for Hawaii." I stared at her in disbelief. She continued, "We already had plans to go there, and I don't see any reason to change them."

I continued to stand there speechless, but my mind screamed, *Don't you want to know how your daughter died? What if her husband played a part in it? Don't you want to greet his parents when they arrive tomorrow from Japan? How can you just pick up and go on with your life as if nothing has happened?* All these thoughts swirled in my head, but I said nothing.

I wondered how Ann would ever gain closure as I thought back to my own father's death and how important I discovered it was to have closure. My parents were divorced when I was in college. Shortly afterwards, my father's business partner died, and so did their business. My father lost his home, his family, and his business all within a short period of time, and he became depressed and despondent.

He accepted the first civil service job that came along and moved to White River, Arizona, to work with the Apache Indians on the reservation.

A week later, my manager at the telephone company, where I worked as a service representative, called me into his office. "I just received a call from White River, Arizona. Your father didn't show up for work today, Kristin. He's missing. His car was found parked on a mountain road—empty."

I collapsed into a chair. A small voice inside told me my father was dead.

The next morning, my manager called. "A scouting group of Apache Indians found your father at the bottom of a 200-foot cliff. I'm sorry, Kristin. Let me know if there's anything I can do."

Although this incident occurred more than 40 years ago, I remember the conversation and the pain like it happened yesterday. Daddy was one of my best friends. We talked openly and honestly with one another. He listened to me and understood my feelings. Plus, he taught me to think for myself. When he and my mother divorced after 22 years of marriage, it was my turn to listen.

After his death, I received a letter he had written the night before he died.

Dear Kristin,
Tomorrow is Saturday. I will pack a picnic lunch and hike up a nearby mountain. It is really beautiful here. I'll take some photographs for you and send them in my next letter....
Love,
Daddy

In time I was able to piece together the details of the fall. Daddy had been hiking along a trail when a soft sandstone ledge gave way below him. His camera, with the promised pictures, was found lying next to him—shattered.

I knew he had been depressed, and many friends and relatives, as well as the insurance company, wondered if he had killed himself. But I knew in my heart he hadn't, and his letter confirmed it in my mind.

This was the first time in my life a situation was so overwhelming that I couldn't handle it by myself. I thanked God for making His presence known to me when I had lost my dearest relative—my precious daddy.

However, I never felt closure. I knew someday I needed to go to White River, but it was 40 years before I was able to fulfill that desire.

When my husband and I finally got the chance, we went to the reservation, to the Bureau of Indian Affairs, and met with an Apache chief. He was able to pull information out of the archives and answer all the questions I had regarding Daddy's work and death. He gave me photocopies of all the papers. I thanked him on behalf of my family for having his tribe scale the dangerous mountain to rescue my father's body.

As we drove away from White River, I squeezed my husband's hand. He gave me a knowing smile, and I realized coming here had given me closure. I leaned back and closed my eyes. My prayer for my sister-in-law, Ann, is that someday she may find closure, too.

☀ ☀ ☀

Words from Jeenie

Eventually, there needs to be a sense of closure—a sense of peace. Some of this may come, as with Kristin, when more details of the death are known. As difficult as it is, there is usually a need to know the full extent of what occurred.

When one chooses to deny and refuses to look with honesty at the death, as did Ann, a healthy outcome will not occur.

Even though pain greatly lessens over time and people go on with their lives, there will always be residual pain. I often explain to my clients that when healing occurs, we are no longer bound by the heavy chain of despair wrapped in a stranglehold around our emotions. However, there will always be residual pain.

This ongoing pain generally will be a moment of pain here and a moment of pain there. We will find we are able to deal with the moments as they arise, because they are fleeting. While some may think that healing equals the total elimination of pain, nothing could be further from the truth.

A moment of pain is palatable. We can embrace it, and it will quickly pass. Even so, we realize healing has occurred.

God's Supply

There are times when we are certain we have no more reserves to call upon. Our tears have fallen on our pillows at night and spring forth at the most inopportune times. In quiet moments we search our souls for a smattering of faith—not sure if it'll be there. We pray, not sure we are being heard. We search for answers—but still they do not come. We dance in a perpetual cycle of grief, and at the lowest point when our hearts feel empty, the unexpected happens: A friend calls with kind words or a Bible verse comes to our minds. Or more dramatically, God sends a message of hope as the sun peeks through dark clouds, and a rainbow appears. Perhaps, after hours of tossing and turning, sleep finally arrives with the beguiling song of a nightingale. God's supply of comfort never runs dry.

In 1 Kings 17 we read of a widow, who God used to supply Elijah with nourishment—a difficult task in the face of utter disaster. Yet it certainly proved the reality that nothing is impossible for God.

As Elijah approached the town gate of Zarephath, he saw a woman busily gathering sticks. Times had been difficult for this widow, and life didn't seem to be getting any better. A drought was ravaging the land, causing hunger, thirst, and a loss of hope. All the widow's resources were gone. Who would provide for her and her son? She looked up as Elijah approached.

> *He called to her and asked, "Would you bring me a little water in a jar so I may have a drink?" As she was going to get it, he called, "And bring me, please, a piece of bread."*
>
> *"As the Lord, your God lives," she replied, "I don't have any bread— only a handful of flour in a jar and a little oil in a jug. I am gathering a few sticks to take home and make a meal for myself and my son, that we may eat it—and die."*
>
> *Elijah said to her, "Don't be afraid. Go home and do as you have said. But first make a small cake of bread for me . . . and then make something for yourself and your son. For this is what the Lord, the God of Israel, says: 'The jar of flour will not be used up and the jug of oil will not run dry until the day the Lord gives rain on the land.'"*
>
> —1 Kings 17:10–14

How sad this poor widow must have felt. She heard Elijah's words, but she had no way of knowing when rain would come. Yet she did exactly as Elijah instructed her.

What would you have done under such outrageous circumstances? Would doubting thoughts haunt you? Would you think, *How foolish this man, Elijah, is. How can I make all he asks out of nothing?*

Imagine the joy she felt when the words of Elijah sprang forth in truth, and her supply of flour and oil miraculously continued— like a fountain never running dry.

As suicide survivors, we, like the widow of Zarephath, soon realize God's supply of comfort never runs dry. On the other side of grief, we'll emerge like a butterfly from its cocoon, rejoicing that God has maintained our faith.

REFLECTIONS

1. Often anger becomes a part of the grief process. Don't hold it in, or it will control you and make it difficult for you to move forward. Journal your angry feelings.

2. Do whatever physical exercise fits into your daily routine. Take daily walks, jog, swim, or if possible join a gym.

3. Beat up a pillow. It sounds silly, but punching a pillow works.

4. Find a peaceful place. Then close your eyes. Imagine you're placing your anger in a box. Wrap the box for overnight express mail—or in this case, "God's Express." Then visualize the package arriving at the throne of God. Ask God to help you let go of the anger, the bitterness, the unresolved questions, etc.

Prayer

Lord, help me to let go of my anger. I know that it won't bring back my loved one. I no longer want my anger to blind me. I don't want it controlling my heart day and night. I want to let go, to laugh, and to feel joy again. I lay all my anger at the foot of Your throne. Please grant me peace. In Jesus's name I pray, amen.

CHAPTER 6

SUICIDE AND DIVORCE: IS THERE A CONNECTION?

"You're blessed when you feel you've lost what is most dear to you.
Only then can you be embraced by the One most dear to you."
—Matthew 5:4 (*The Message*)

Separated and divorced people readily acknowledge that suicidal thoughts often cross their minds. The thought, *I can't live through this,* can be constant.

One morning Tara's husband, looking tired and tense, walked into the kitchen. Deep circles had formed under his eyes. He sat down at the breakfast table and said, "I care about you, but I don't love you enough to live with you anymore."

After 22 years of marriage, Tara's world crumbled. She realized her relationship with Bill was strained, but she didn't dream that he wanted a divorce. With those words, Tara knew her marriage was dead, and a part of her died with it since so much of her life revolved around her husband.

Emotionally, she fell into a deep pit. She reached a point where she was too stressed to pray and too fragmented to read the Bible. It was impossible for her to reach out and call on God during this period when she needed Him most. God seemed distant and silent.

She wanted her situation changed, her problems solved, although she was unable to do anything to alter her circumstances. Her poor mental attitude was having a negative effect on her children. They, too, suffered from the pending divorce. Yet, she didn't have the reserves to comfort them or quell their doubts and fears. There were times when she didn't want to face the future—the next day, the next week, the next year...

Jeenie gives another example of the devastating effect divorce can have—this time from the husband's viewpoint.

Aaron's Pit
Jeenie Gordon

He was in his late 20s, good-looking enough to be a movie star. Intelligent, with a vibrant personality, he could capture a heart in a minute—but his world fell apart.

Aaron stumbled into my office, and tears cascaded down his sculptured face like a giant waterfall. Slumping into the sofa, between the sobs, he told me his story of pain. I listened carefully.

Married a few short years to his beautiful dream girl, he thought life was blissful—until today.

"Angela wants out of our marriage. Her bags are packed, and she is ready to walk out of the door and out of my life forever."

"I'm sorry to hear that, Aaron. Tell me what happened."

"Angela was swept off her feet by an older, married man at work. The more she spoke of his amazing attributes, the more my heart disintegrated. That's why I decided to seek counseling."

During the next few weeks, I was supportive and caring toward this broken man. Returning home late one evening, I had numerous messages from him.

"Jeenie, I need you. Please pick up. Jeenie, I can't stand the pain, and I'm going to end it."

With a loaded gun and a broken heart, he called for help. My heart was nearly beating out of my chest as I dialed his number.

"Please, God," I prayed, "Let him still be alive."

Thankfully he answered, and I was able to talk him through the night.

Years later, Aaron remarried a wonderful Christian woman, had children, and today is involved in ministry to others in despair.

Not all stories turn out as well as Aaron's. The dark well of emotion surrounds many people in marital trauma as they sink into a pit of deep muck, unable to climb out. Often they do not possess enough strength to grab onto a lifesaving rope.

Just as Aaron is able to help others today, Richard was able to save a friend's life because he understood the emotions she was going through.

"Mom, I've Been There"
Susan Titus Osborn

I watched Richard race down the stairs, shoving his brother, Mike, out of the way. He had a wild look in his eyes that scared me. I had never seen my son behave like that before. As he brushed past me on the way to the front door, I saw a Buck knife in his hand. By the time I reached the door, he had jumped in my car and was driving away.

Mike and I stared at each other for a moment, and then Mike turned and walked slowly back up the stairs. Moments later, he cried, "Mom, you'd better come look at this."

I ran up the stairs and grabbed the paper my youngest son was holding out to me. It read, "I can't go on any longer. Please forgive me. Richard."

Sinking down on Richard's bed, I began to cry. Mike sat down and put his arms around me.

"I had no idea Richard was depressed. Did you?"

"No, Mom. I know his girlfriend broke up with him, but that's happened before."

I added, "And you made the varsity water polo team, and he didn't. That had to be hard for him." Mike was a freshman, the only one on varsity. Richard, a junior, was still playing on junior varsity.

I took Mike's hands and prayed, "Lord, please bring Richard safely home to us." Throughout the next few hours, I prayed that prayer over and over. I felt so stressed I couldn't get beyond that one sentence.

My husband was on a business trip, so I called the hotel where he said he was staying in Philadelphia. The clerk said no one was registered by that name. We were struggling in our marriage, so I wasn't surprised my husband wasn't where he said he would be. The tension in our home had been hard on the boys, too. I realized that, but didn't know what to do about it.

I sat at my dining room table, praying now and then, but mostly just staring off into space. Finally, about four in the morning, the front door opened, and in walked Richard, head down, knife at his side.

He put the knife on the table and said, "I couldn't do it, Mom. I couldn't take my own life. God wouldn't let me."

I stood up and wrapped my arms around my firstborn. I silently prayed, *Thank You, Lord.*

My husband and I divorced shortly thereafter. I never did figure out where he was that terrible night, but somehow Richard had found out his father was cheating on me. So for over a year he carried around that burden, as well as the problems he had at school.

Once everything came out in the open, Richard's life settled down. The incident was forgotten for six years until one night when the telephone rang, and Richard said, "Mom, I'm so glad you're home. I need to talk to you. Brittney tried to commit suicide last night, but I stopped her."

"Richard, do you want me to stop by your place on the way to work? I'd be happy to."

He replied, "No, Mom. That's OK. I just want to talk for a while."

"Take all the time you need. Tell me what happened."

A few months earlier, Richard had helped his friend, Brittney, through a difficult time in her life. Her parents had divorced, and since he had gone through that, he could empathize. He encouraged her to see a psychologist for her depression and drug problem. He thought she was doing much better—until the previous night.

Richard continued, "Brittney left a message on my machine. I had checked my messages earlier, but an inner voice told me to check them again."

"You know Who that was, don't you?" I asked, never missing an opportunity to witness to my jet-setting son who rarely took time to go to church.

"Oh, Mom, I know you pray for me all the time. You've told me you pray that angels will surround me and protect me." He added softly, "I guess this time they really did. If she had died, I would have felt so guilty and would have wondered if I could have done more for her. All my life I would have carried that burden."

"No way would it have been your fault if she had died, but thankfully, you were able to stop her. Now tell me what happened."

Richard continued, "I checked my messages a second time, and there was one new one—from Brittney. Her voice sounded groggy, distant. I knew something was terribly wrong. I knew—I had been there… I told my roommate, and we rushed to her house. Later we found out she had taken an overdose of painkillers, downed a bottle of wine, and taken some other drugs."

I interrupted my son, "Is she going to be all right?"

"The doctor said she would have died if we had not found her when we did. I'm so thankful I checked my answering machine a second time. I rarely do that."

Richard and I talked for about an hour—about his dealing with the situation, what he could do, and what he needed to leave in God's hands. At the end of the conversation, Richard said, "Mom, I'm glad I caught you before you left this morning. It helps to know you're there."

"I'll always be here for you—no matter what."

⚛︎ ⚛︎ ⚛︎

Words from Jeenie

Suicide is often a silent killer. Satan takes control over a person's heart and emotions, feeding them with a truckload of lies—over and over—saying things such as: "Life's just not worth living. No one really cares for you. They won't even miss you. Things will never be better. You might just as well end it. Here's how."

1 Peter 5:8 states, *"Be self-controlled and alert. Your enemy the devil prowls around like a roaring lion looking for someone to devour."*

Lions silently wait, watching their prey from a distance, making no sudden moves. Stealthily they creep closer and closer to their intended victim, who is blithely unaware. Then, in a flash, the reigning king of the wild pounces on his prey. With gigantic teeth, he rips into the jugular vein and conquers.

Only the Lion of Judah can conquer the forces of evil, as He did for Richard and Brittney. This story greatly exhibits the power of prayer.

I truly believe none of us will know the magnitude, potency, and weight of our prayers, until someday when we stand face-to-face with our Lord and Savior, Jesus Christ.

Joy in Life
C. A. N.

I'm finding joy in life again
Taking it day-by-day,
Doing things I like to do,
And spending quality time with me.

I was lost for many months,
Forgetting who I was.
Life was empty and meaningless,
I wanted to end it all.

Deeper and deeper I fell
Into a big dark hole,
Unable to get out on my own.
Could anyone hear me yell?

I cried out to You for help;
I couldn't do it on my own.
The hole began to close in on me.
I had all but drowned.

You threw me a rope,
Hoping to save my life,
But I kept falling deeper,
Thinking nothing could ever be right.

One day I finally caught
The rope You had thrown in.
The rope was Jesus Christ.
I then knew I could win.

I can rejoice in life again,
Happy to be alive,

Thankful to my friends and God,
That I did not die.

So I've been making it a point
To cherish me, myself, and I,
And treat myself as valuable—
Choosing to live, not die.

———

So far, the people in this chapter have chosen life over death. In the following story, however, Erik's papa was emotionally unable to survive a separation and pending divorce. As a result, the lives of those left behind were shattered—forever.

Erik's Papa
Jeanne Pallos

I knew about hurting hearts and how God could use safe, loving, caring people to bring healing. He had done it in my life. In return, I longed to reach into the hearts of emotionally wounded children and minister with God's love and grace. So I started a class at church for children with hurting hearts. The staff knew I wasn't a trained counselor, nor did I pretend to be, but they agreed to allow God to direct me.

Erik's mother pleaded with me to let him into the class. "He's seen so much pain in his short life," she said. "At five years old, Erik lost his dad to suicide. He needs to be in your class."

Even though Erik was only eight, and the other children were fourth- through sixth-graders, how could I say no? I thought, *Love and support is what all these children need.* "I'll be happy to take Erik into my class."

The first week, a shy little boy, with his head down, walked into the classroom. We sat in one large circle, and Erik took the seat next to mine. Although I knew the personal tragedies in each child's life, I never mentioned them. I vowed never to pry into a child's heart.

Erik rarely spoke, but at the beginning of each class, he scurried to sit next to me. One week I asked the children to make collages depicting people and things they loved. We searched through magazines and collected pictures. Then the children disappeared into their own private worlds as they cut and pasted pictures and words onto large sheets of paper.

Since Erik was the youngest, I often helped him with projects. As we sat pasting a picture of a father and son tossing a ball, he said, "Papa liked to play ball with me."

Erik had never mentioned his dad before.

"That must have been fun and made you very happy."
I silently prayed, *Thank You, God, for working in Erik's heart.*

The next week, during the class activity, Erik whispered to me, "Papa used to read to me."

"That sounds so special," I replied. "I'm sure your papa loved reading to you."

A few weeks later, just before Christmas, our church held its annual memorial service. Families brought pictures of loved ones to display on a table and wrote the deceased person's name on a list to be read. During the service, each family walked forward to light a candle.

I walked forward and placed my mother's picture on the table. Suddenly, I noticed Erik walking toward me. He looked up at me with expressive eyes.

"Do you want to see Papa?" he asked.

"Oh, yes," I answered, taking his small hand. "I'd love to see your papa."

Together, we found Papa's picture—a snapshot of a man and a child secured in a cracked frame.

"Is that you?" I asked.

Erik smiled.

"I can tell your papa loved you very much. Do you want to see a picture of my mother?" I asked.

When the evening ended, Erik's mother took me aside and told me the details of the suicide. "Erik's dad and I were separated. He lived alone. One evening he phoned and threatened, 'I'm climbing onto a chair and making a noose. I'm going to kill myself.'

"I pleaded with him, 'Please get some counseling. Your kids will always need you.' Then I heard a thud, and the conversation ended in an overpowering silence."

I wanted to say something comforting, but couldn't find the words. As I looked into her eyes, I saw sadness, but I also saw determination. Widowed, and left with three heartbroken children, she'd not given up.

Had my class touched Erik's young heart? Could the love he received in a few short weeks bring healing for a lifetime? I knew it couldn't, but it was a beginning.

Erik loved his papa, no matter how he had died. That's all that mattered. Erik now needed me and others to listen, care, and affirm this love. This little boy had a lifetime to deal with his papa's suicide. For now he needed help in treasuring his dad's memory before it faded away.

☀ ☀ ☀

Words from Jeenie

In a moment of insanity, Erik's father did not consider what his act would do to his family. He was merely trying to escape the racking, wrenching pain.

Erik's mother was determined to survive. She was certain her family in God's strength would get through this together. Healing is always a choice, but often it won't begin until the first year of mourning has passed. Nevertheless, it will come.

Choosing to survive, determining to be happy again, and trusting in the goodness of God will determine the quality of one's future.

Two Disciples—Different Choices

Both Peter and Judas Iscariot were Jesus's disciples. They had climbed the Judean hills with Him, heard Him speak to thousands, and watched as He healed the sick, opened blind eyes, and made the lame walk. But there the similarity ends.

Judas Iscariot was selfish and self-serving. As keeper of the money bag, he helped himself to its contents. Perhaps the reason he betrayed Christ was due to his preconceived idea of who Jesus as the Messiah should be—a conquering hero. When Jesus didn't meet those expectations, he took action.

> *Then one of the Twelve—the one called Judas Iscariot—went to the chief priests and asked, "What are you willing to give me if I hand him over to you?" So they counted out for him thirty silver coins. From then on Judas watched for an opportunity to hand him over.*
> —Matthew 26:14–16

That opportunity came when Jesus was in the garden of Gethsemane, a place Jesus often met with His disciples and one Judas knew well. Judas came to the garden, leading a detachment of soldiers and some officials from the chief priests and Pharisees. When Judas pointed out Jesus, they arrested Him. Yet later, Judas regretted his actions and tried to undo them, but it was too late.

> *When Judas, who had betrayed him, saw that Jesus was condemned, he was seized with remorse and returned the thirty silver coins to the chief priests and the elders.*
> *"I have sinned," he said, "for I have betrayed innocent blood."*
> *"What is that to us?" they replied. "That's your responsibility."*
> *So Judas threw the money into the temple and left. Then he went away and hanged himself.*
> —Matthew 27:3–5

As well as predicting Judas Iscariot's betrayal, Jesus also knew Peter would disown Him and told him so in Matthew 26:33–35.

> Peter replied, "Even if all fall away on account of you, I never will."
> "I tell you the truth," Jesus answered, "this very night, before the rooster crows, you will disown me three times."
> But Peter declared, "Even if I have to die with you, I will never disown you." And all the other disciples said the same.

When Jesus was arrested and taken to the house of the high priest, Peter followed at a distance. He entered the courtyard and sat down with the guards around a fire.

> A servant girl saw him seated there in the firelight. She looked closely at him and said, "This man was with him."
> But he denied it. "Woman, I don't know him," he said.
> A little later someone else saw him and said, "You also are one of them."
> "Man, I am not!" Peter replied.
> About an hour later another asserted, "Certainly this fellow was with him, for he is a Galilean."
> Peter replied, "Man, I don't know what you're talking about!" Just as he was speaking, the rooster crowed. The Lord turned and looked straight at Peter. Then Peter remembered the word the Lord had spoken to him: "Before the rooster crows today, you will disown me three times." And he went outside and wept bitterly.
> —Luke 22:56–62

In time, Peter repented, accepted God's forgiveness, and renewed his commitment to follow Jesus. (See John 21:15–19.) He became a respected and godly leader of the early church, authored two books of the Bible, and served Jesus with his entire heart. Both Judas Iscariot and Peter made choices, but only one chose well.

In the following story, Anne tells of the devastating effect her divorce had on her children.

No Turning Back
Anne Wilson

Over the years I have finally accepted that I might not have all the answers to my questions regarding the suicide of my son. It has been difficult to face some of the issues that I believe contributed to his death. I know that his dad and I both miss him and grieve over the loss of our son. That our divorce may have been a contributing factor in his suicide is still difficult to face.

Perhaps, our story will serve to prevent another suicide and save a life. I hope so. When I think of my son, Ken, I see a tall young man with deep expressive eyes, who remained childlike in so many ways. Emotionally he never overcame the divorce of his parents.

I'll never forget the day I had to tell Ken his dad had moved out. He'd been on a weekend camping trip with his Boy Scout troop. I felt grateful our teenage son and daughter hadn't been home the night their dad left.

The next morning when I drove to pick up Ken, my hands shook. I prayed, "Lord, please help me to tell Ken in a gentle way. Help him to know he is loved."

I pulled into the parking lot where we were to meet our sons. There was an excitement in the air. I watched as teenage boys with sleeping bags tucked under their arms and backpacks over their shoulders said goodbye to one another. Scouts from several troops had come together for this campout. I spotted Ken waving to some other boys. He had a big grin on his face. At 14, he looked older than his age and stood a foot taller than me. Suddenly, he saw our car and headed in my direction.

Tears formed, but I quickly wiped them away. I knew our world had changed, and I had to be the bearer of news that would bring pain. On the way home he told me about the campout.

As we pulled into the driveway Ken asked, "Mom, is Dad home from his business trip?"

"Ken, your dad has moved out." Without a word he got out of the car, turned, and walked toward the front door. Once inside he went directly to his room. There he remained until I knocked on his door and said, "It's time to go pick up Leanne. The youth group is back from their camping trip."

Ken's bedroom door opened. He stepped out looking pale and stared straight ahead. Ken remained silent all the way to the church parking lot where we picked up Leanne.

I spotted her standing next to her counselor. Her face looked swollen and red. She'd been crying.

I hugged her and asked, "Leanne, what's wrong?"

"I talked with Dad. I know that he's divorcing you."

"When did you talk with him?"

"Yesterday, I called home. Dad told me you weren't there. Then he said he'd stopped by for some more of his belongings."

With her arm around Leanne, her counselor added, "She cried all night."

"Leanne, I'm sorry."

Later, at home, I could see the pain etched across both of their faces. I said, "It's OK to feel angry. You both can tell me how you feel." But Ken just shook his head and went to his room.

Leanne and I sat together in the living room and talked. She said, "Six months ago I heard you and Dad arguing. I felt scared you might divorce, especially when Dad talked about another woman. But then things seemed better—until now. Mom, what's going to happen to us?"

"Leanne, I'm sorry for all the pain. It'll be hard, but we'll be OK."

Before our separation I'd been thrilled to have an outstanding progress report from Ken's special education teacher and counselor. They'd said, "Mrs. Wilson, Ken has shown great improvement this quarter. His comprehension and ability to complete assignments has increased."

Then after our divorce, everything changed, and Ken's depression manifested itself in both his schoolwork and home life.

He refused to talk about his pain. And I hoped he'd find the determination to move forward after he was hospitalized twice for depression.

Do I believe that our divorce played a role in my son's suicide? Yes, I do. Young people need both parents for guidance and support. Divorce forced me to give up my role as a stay-at-home mom. I worked 12 hours a day on weekdays and every other weekend.

Both Ken and Leanne knew that every other weekend they were supposed to be with their dad, but he never followed through. Leanne expressed her anger by saying, "I wouldn't go anyway." But once again, Ken did not express his feelings. Although I didn't speak negatively about their dad, they felt his absence.

Leanne suffered, too, but she had the strength to climb over many obstacles. She has matured into a beautiful woman with a family and career of her own. I am proud of her.

Yet, she often tells me, "I miss my brother."

That's when I put my arms around her and say, "We all do."

⁂ ⁂ ⁂

For divorced parents Anne's advice is, "Work together for the emotional needs of your children. Tell them often how much they are loved. If they seem depressed, seek professional counseling. If you say you will spend a day or a weekend with them, make sure you follow through."

Words from Jeenie

Having counseled thousands of teens in high school, I know that divorce is a common but severe trauma. Rarely did I have a year go by that I did not look into the face of a teen surrounded in satin and encompassed in a casket. Many times the breaking point was his or her parents' divorce.

Leanne often talked about her feelings to her mother, her counselor, and probably her friends. She did not hide her grief, but was open and honest, allowing herself to feel the pain.

Ken, however, buried his pain deep within himself—a common male response. He locked himself into an emotional prison, one with iron bars too strong for him to emerge—or so he thought.

Since teenage boys desperately need to learn masculinity from their father, much of Ken's identify as a male died when his father left. Silently he suffered. When the pain became more than he could stand, he decided he could not go on.

Repressing emotional anguish can be deadly, but let's remember those special words of Corrie ten Boom's sister Betsie: *There is no pit so deep that He is not deeper still.*

REFLECTIONS

1. Describe positive ways you can grieve the loss of your marriage and overcome depression.

2. Describe positive ways you can reassure your young children (or teenagers or even adult children) that you and your spouse both love them.

Prayer

Lord, I feel so alone. Remove the despair and hopelessness. I need to feel Your presence and regain my hope in a future. Use each incident in my life to strengthen my faith. In Jesus's name I pray, amen.

CHAPTER 7

GOD, HELP ME!

The Lord is close to the brokenhearted
and saves those who are crushed in spirit.
—Psalm 34:18

At the age of 13, Louise fell out of her dad's boat. She knew how to swim, but the icy cold water took her breath away, and the thick reeds, growing up from the bottom of the lake, wrapped around her legs. She panicked as she gasped for air and gulped water. Hopelessness and doubt kept her focused on fear, and she could not free herself. She fought to stay above the water. Silently she prayed, *God help me!*

Suddenly, she felt someone beside her—a man pulling the reeds away from her. He said, "Louise, you're safe now." He gave her a shove toward shore.

To her surprise, just a short distance away from where she had struggled, her feet touched bottom and she walked ashore. There she found loving, compassionate people ready to help her.

Louise thought, *What would have happened if I hadn't cried out for help? What would have happened if a stranger hadn't cared enough to swim out to help me? In the murky water I couldn't see the bottom of the lake. Safety had been only a few feet away.*

So it is in the throes of depression. The suicidal person can't see through the murkiness of her pain to know that safety lies only a short distance away.

Suicide is never a good option. It does not solve anything. It brings an abrupt end to the resources that could have brought relief, completion of fulfilled dreams, and the return of happiness.

There are a number of mental disorders that cause chemical imbalances in the brain and may contribute to suicidal behavior. However, they can often be controlled with medication when prescribed and overseen by a psychiatrist. Although these illnesses are often treatable, some emotionally desperate patients will choose not to live.

Often external circumstances such as job loss, financial disaster, loss of a child, failure in school, or marital problems are blamed for suicide. However, these events may act only as triggers. In a moment where reality is lost, suicide occurs.

Shame overwhelmingly surrounds a suicide. Society does not accept it in the same way as dying from a dreaded physical disease. Nonetheless, suicide represents horrific illness, one of the emotions and mind.

In previous chapters we've read about the aftermath of suicide. We realize that Christians are not immune from depression and often lose loved ones to suicide. In this chapter we are going to look at another aspect of suicide. Many Christians during stressful, hurtful times contemplate suicide. For some, they believe the turnaround came when they called out in distress, "God help me."

These words are often the beginning of a path to recovery for those contemplating suicide. God becomes to them a safe harbor. In seeking help from professionals (support groups, pastors, family physicians, and Christian therapists), they explore the reasons behind their pain. With the love and mercy of a sovereign God, they grab hold of a life preserver—the choice to live.

For others, in a moment of desperation they call out to God, unsure of His existence. And, for many, that is the defining moment when God becomes real and personal to them, making suicide no longer an option.

In the next story Kathy struggles with suicidal thoughts, but her love for Jesus becomes her life preserver.

I Almost Took My Life
Kathy Collard Miller

As the train rumbled past the East Coast countryside, my thoughts were as piercing as the screeching wheels of the train. *Why did Greg kill himself?* He was a distant relative whom I rarely saw, yet the news of Greg's suicide made tears fill my eyes. *Oh, to be that full of despair.*

In the past I'd struggled with suicidal feelings. I glanced over at my 28-year-old sleeping daughter. If I had acted on those feelings, I wouldn't have the fabulous mother-daughter relationship I now enjoy with Darcy.

But 26 years earlier, my depression and life had careened out of control. Larry and I had celebrated our seventh anniversary, but it wasn't a happy occasion. Unwisely, I asked again, "Larry, why do you work so many hours? Having a two-year-old and a newborn is hard work. I need you to help me."

"Kathy, I try to help you. Being a policeman is demanding. I'm working all those hours to secure our financial future."

I knew I'd spoiled our time together. Silence again surrounded us, and a fog of hopelessness encircled me. My thoughts turned inward. *Kathy, you never do anything right. Larry hates you.* Then in my own defense, I mentally screamed, *I hate him too.* Doubts and fear haunted me. *Will we get a divorce? Why can't we talk? We used to be in love.* Then I prayed silently, *Lord, we're Christians. We're not supposed to act like this. What's wrong?*

Often I prayed for my marriage and my angry reactions to our 2-year-old daughter. My anger toward Darcy escalated when I felt rejected by Larry. Her strong-willed nature resisted toilet training and resulted in constant temper tantrums that wore me down. Constantly I yelled at her. But that wasn't all. My reactions had deteriorated into angry spanking, kicking, and pushing, and I felt totally powerless to stop my behavior.

"O God, help me," I cried. When my rage increased and prayers went unanswered, I concluded God had given up on me.

The day after our disastrous anniversary dinner, I caught Darcy playing in the fireplace ashes. I exploded, "Darcy, how many times must I tell you not to play in the fireplace?" I ran over to her and screamed again and again as I choked her. In my frenzy, it was as if I left my body and was watching a horrible movie of a crazed woman, choking a little blonde-headed toddler.

Then within seconds, I was back in my right mind, and I jerked my hands away from Darcy's throat. She gasped for air and began screaming. I ran down the hall, trying to escape the horrible scene. "O God, I don't deserve to live."

I slammed my bedroom door behind me. *I'm a terrible mother. I can't believe I did that.*

Then I remembered what Larry had said before he left for work. "Kathy, I'm leaving my off-duty service revolver in the top dresser drawer today because I don't need it. Don't let Darcy get close to it."

That's the answer—Larry's gun. A tiny voice in my head sinisterly whispered, *Take your life. God doesn't care. Otherwise He would instantaneously deliver you from your anger and heal your marriage. There's nothing for you to live for.*

With trembling hands, I opened the top dresser drawer, and the gleam from the shiny barrel of the gun glinted at me invitingly. Darcy's crying from the other room wrenched my heart. *She's better off without me. I've ruined her for life.*

I stared at the gun and began to reach into the drawer. But then a new thought suddenly entered my mind. *What will people think of Jesus if they hear that Kathy Miller has taken her own life?*

My hand stopped. The faces of the women in the neighborhood Bible study that I led flitted before me. My family members who didn't know Christ came to mind. I thought of my unsaved neighbors whom I had witnessed to.

O Lord, I don't care about my reputation, but I do care about Yours. I call myself a Christian, and so many people know it. What will they think about You if I use this gun?

The concern for Jesus's reputation saved my life that day, and I knew it was prompted by the Holy Spirit. I didn't have any hope at that point, but in the following months, God proved Himself faithful by revealing the underlying causes of my anger. He gave me patience to be a loving mom and then healed my relationship with Larry.

Suddenly, my reverie snapped back to the present as the train began slowing for the next stop. I looked over at my daughter who had awakened and was gazing out the window, and I smiled. The thought struck me forcefully, *If I had taken my life, I would have missed: Darcy's wedding three years ago and our son's graduation from college. I wouldn't have had the opportunities to speak in 29 states and five foreign countries or to have written 47 books.*

The list went on and on. I thought of Larry who is my best friend and our 35 years of marriage. If I'd used the gun that day, Larry probably would have remarried. And I knew my daughter and son would have grieved over a missing mother who seemed to be more absorbed in her own pain than about their welfare.

Yes, I understood how Greg could have so little hope that he took his life. But I wish I could have shared with him that there's always hope, and God is faithful if we will hold on to Him and His promises. I'm so grateful I did.

My daughter turned to me and said, "Mom, I'm so excited we're spending a vacation together in New York City."

※ ※ ※

Words from Jeenie

Satan was out to destroy Kathy's life—her children, husband, and future ministry. She almost fell prey to the lies he fed her through her thoughts and emotions. Thanks be to God, she did not succumb.

As a therapist and Christian, I believe Satan's main job with believers is to kill and destroy. He attacks us ferociously with fears, depression, and negative thought patterns. His words always have a snippet of truth, which we often swallow. *Yeah, that's right!* we think.

The kicker is that following the tidbit of truth is the huge lie. We tend to swallow it hook, line, and sinker. And at that point, he has us in his demonic grip, and he can and does oppress us.

However, our God is more powerful than Satan. *"You, dear children, are from God and have overcome them, because the one who is in you is greater than the one who is in the world"* (I John 4:4).

WHO CARES
Charles R. Brown

Indigo days.
Dark, deep sea nights,
Layer upon layer,
The grays of life
Are pressed into strips
Of midnight black.
Dilated irises stretch wide,
Thirsty for the smallest flicker of light.

Can't see.
Can't see any purpose in it at all.
I can't tell if my eyelids are open or shut.
All I know is my life is shut.
The door has closed, the key thrown away.
Cold dungeon walls
Leave bruises on the mind.
Silence offers no peace—only fear.
The slamming in my chest
Rattles any semblance of sanity.
Why?
Who cares anyway?
No one will miss me.
They'll be better off when I'm gone.

Is anyone listening?

———

MISGUIDED

Sometimes when God tells Christians to go in one direction, they go in the opposite. The story of Jonah demonstrates this problem. Jonah's hatred for people who were known enemies of Israel and his own preconceived notions of justice caused him to disobey God when he was told to go to Nineveh.

> But Jonah ran away from the Lord and headed for Tarshish. He went down to Joppa, where he found a ship bound for that port. After paying the fare, he went aboard and sailed for Tarshish to flee from the Lord.
> —Jonah 1:3

Let's put our imaginations to work and board the ship with Jonah. Feel the sea breeze and hear the rushing sound of waves as the ship sails along. Watch Jonah. He seems anxious, and every nerve in his body is on edge. When exhaustion overtakes him, he goes below deck and sleeps. Momentarily, sleep allows Jonah to escape his thoughts and fears. Then suddenly the panicked ship's captain startles him awake. *"How can you sleep? Get up and call on your god! Maybe he will take notice of us, and we will not perish"* (Jonah 1:6).

Instantly, Jonah realized God brought a raging storm because of his disobedience. *"'Pick me up and throw me into the sea,' he replied, 'and it will become calm. I know that it is my fault that this great storm has come upon you'"* (Jonah 1:12).

As soon as Jonah's body hit the turbulent sea, the storm ceased. Encased in a tomb of darkness, surrounded by slime and a bad stench, Jonah knew a huge fish had swallowed him.

He cried out to God. *"When my life was ebbing away, I remembered you, Lord, and my prayer rose to you, to your holy temple"* (Jonah 2:7).

After three days God ordered the fish to vomit up Jonah. Finally Jonah obeyed God and traveled to Nineveh to tell the people to repent. The people of Nineveh believed God's message and obeyed. God responded to their change of heart and showed mercy to them.

Yet, instead of rejoicing with God, Jonah became angry. He'd not learned the lesson of mercy and forgiveness. Jonah 4:2–3 gives us a clear picture of his preconceived thoughts. *"I knew that you are a gracious and compassionate God, slow to anger and abounding in love, a God who relents from sending calamity. Now, O Lord, take away my life, for it is better for me to die than to live."*

Jonah obviously missed the point. He sat under a makeshift shelter, allowing his thoughts to control him as he spiraled deeper into despair.

God taught Jonah another lesson in mercy and compassion. He allowed a vine to grow and provide shade for Jonah. Then overnight God sent a worm to destroy the vine. The next day the sun beat down on Jonah and made him faint.

> *But God said to Jonah, "Do you have a right to be angry about the vine?"*
> *"I do," he said, "I am angry enough to die."*
> *But the Lord said, "You have been concerned about this vine, though you did not tend it or make it grow. It sprang up overnight and died overnight. But Nineveh has more than a hundred and twenty thousand*

people who cannot tell their right hand from their left, and many cattle as well. Should I not be concerned about that great city?"
—Jonah 4:9-11

What a unique way for the Creator of all heaven and earth to teach a man about his misguided thoughts. The lessons Jonah learned are wise choices for us today.

- To trust God.
- To obey God.
- To show others compassion and mercy.

Terry shares how his heart attack, followed by a deep depression, changed the direction of his life. When his suicidal thoughts reached a no-return point, something amazing happened.

Call Upon Me
Terry Temple

As senior lieutenant assistant chief of police, I commanded both the patrol and detective divisions. I'd earned several awards: National Citation for Bravery, Certificate of Valor, and a resolution from the state senate for bravery. In addition to being selected as one of the "Top Ten Cops" in the entire US, I received my police department's Medal of Valor. I'd worked hard. One position away from being at the top of my chosen profession, my life couldn't get much better. Then it all came to an end.

I'd been working in my office, when I suddenly felt pressure in my chest. I stood up and walked into the adjoining office of the other division commander. Jim looked up and said, "Sit down, Terry. You look awful."

"It must be indigestion," I replied.

"I'm calling the paramedics."

I started to protest, but then the pain hit. A short time later, they rushed me to the hospital with an IV in my arm and the ambulance's siren blaring. Once in the emergency room, the doctor told me, "You've had a heart attack."

Twelve days later they released me. For the next eight months of my disability leave, I enjoyed unlimited free time—no pressure, no deadlines, no stack of overdue staff work. I felt convinced I had the world by the tail. Disability pay was 100 percent with zero deductions. It had a strange effect on me. I bought a new travel trailer, a new Dodge Ram Charger, and lots of expensive things.

My disability retirement became official in December of 1982. As the months passed, I became increasingly bored. I thought, *I feel worthless as a man.*

I began to drink to dull the pain, and the primary recipients of my unhappiness were those closest to me—my wife and teenage daughter. They took the brunt of my boozing and unreasonableness.

I dabbled in several areas of employment. None of which satisfied me. Finally, a good friend introduced me to another retired policeman. Lee had started a private investigation business. "Terry, come work for me as a private investigator," he offered.

Soon I learned that being a PI did not come close to the excitement of being a cop. I hated it. As a compromise, I decided to go to polygraph school in San Diego. The course lasted seven weeks. After graduation, I returned to Lee's private investigation firm as a lie detector technician. However, changes in the polygraph profession severely cut back business. Bills became overdue. Threats of repossession began to show up in our mailbox, including a foreclosure notice on our home.

Then one morning at work, the phone rang. My boss wanted an update on the complicated case I'd been assigned. As I picked up the file to review it, I overheard two of my co-workers in the hallway, discussing something about the Bible. I listened, and feeling curious, I walked out of my office to join them. I followed them to a rear office and sat down. Steve asked, "Terry, do you know Jesus?"

"I've never been real religious."

"Terry, it's not about religion. It's about a personal relationship with the Son of God," replied Tom.

"How could He change my life?" I responded.

"Why don't you join our weekly Bible study?" Steve asked.

"I'll think it over."

Back in my office, my mind screamed, *I've got to get away from everything.*

I quickly packed my belongings and strode out of the building. As I climbed into my car I thought, *I can't deal with life anymore.*

When I drove toward the freeway, memories of my heart attack flooded my mind. I glanced out the window at the slow-moving traffic. I glanced up at the dark storm clouds overhead and spiraled down even deeper into my depression. I thought, *I have no future. The only answer is to end it all. It's two in the afternoon. My wife and daughter aren't home yet. I'll hook up our 18-foot travel trailer and split for some secluded spot in the desert. After inhaling a case or so of beer, I'll eat my gun.*

Tears streamed down my cheeks as concealed emotions surfaced. I burst into uncontrollable weeping. Between gasps for air, I cried, "God, I need You. I've blown it! I can't go another step without You!"

In that moment something happened—something real— something I will never forget. Just when I thought I'd go over the edge, a tangible calm came over me. Inside my car, the air became comfortably warm and cozy. I felt my heavy burdens begin to lift. For the first time in more than two years, my fear vanished. I felt at peace. Within seconds I understood. "God, You're real!"

With my heart screaming for forgiveness, I cried, "God, I surrender my life to You."

From that moment on, the Lord began to transform me. My family life became full again as my wife and daughter forgave me. Together we rejoiced, knowing God was true to His promise—a promise made long ago. We can read about it in Jeremiah 33:3: *"Call to me and I will answer you and tell you great and unsearchable things you do not know."*

I share my story in the hope that my experience will reach others who have given up on life and who need God in their lives. Eighteen years have passed, and I don't regret one single moment of my life in Jesus. You won't either!

☀ ☀ ☀

Words from Jeenie

Deep within the heart of a man is the desire to provide for and protect his family. Because of that, the vast majority of a male's self-worth often comes from his job. If work is going well, he will feel good about himself.

Terry's newfound freedom and pressure-free lifestyle was utopia—for a time. Soon, however, life no longer had meaning. New jobs did not meet his expectations. He realized he wasn't providing enough income for his family and could possibly face financial ruin, thus, adding to his feeling of worthlessness.

Not seeing a life preserver or means of escape, he quickly sank into a watery abyss. Without Christ there is no hope of rescue. We must allow Him to embrace us and carry us to safety. Grabbing hold of Jesus, Terry accepted his rescue from sin. Then he relaxed in the arms of his Savior and was carried to a secure haven.

Numerous times I've stated to clients, "Although I believe in therapy, Jesus is the true answer!"

REFLECTIONS

1. Often our fears and thoughts keep us from reaching out for help. Do you have any preconceived thoughts that keep you from trusting God?

2. Ask God in prayer to show you the plan He has for your life.

Prayer

Lord, help me to stop running from You. Teach me to say no to bad thoughts and give me the ability to seek help. Place me on a path that brings wholeness. In Jesus's name I pray, amen.

CHAPTER 8

ON THE EDGE

So we fix our eyes not on what is seen, but on what is unseen.
For what is seen is temporary, but what is unseen is eternal.
—2 Corinthians 4:18

Kim's parents had been yelling at each other when her mom grabbed Kim's arm and said, "Come on. I'm taking you to Uncle Kevin's mountain cabin." Mom packed so quickly that Kim left her favorite doll behind, and she always took Baby Doll with her wherever she went.

Kim felt strangely insecure as Mom drove in silence up the winding road. Kim normally loved visiting Aunt Jane and Uncle Kevin, but this time she had an uneasy feeling that her four-year-old mind couldn't comprehend. When they arrived, Mom seemed in a hurry to leave. She quickly hugged Kim, kissed her cheek, and said, "Be a good girl." This made Kim feel even more uncomfortable.

Aunt Jane and Uncle Kevin whispered a lot after Mom left, but when Kim looked at them, they quickly stopped talking. After a few days, Kim felt terribly homesick, but she didn't know how to tell them, so she started acting out.

Once at naptime, she pulled feathers out of her pillow and stuffed them into her suitcase. It helped to relieve her frustrations a little. But when Aunt Jane opened Kim's suitcase to find her sweater, feathers flew all over the place. "Kim, why'd you do this? No dessert for you tonight."

Kim just shrugged her shoulders. She didn't have an answer.

The cabin sat nestled among pine trees close to a cliff. A fence Uncle Kevin built ran along the edge. Aunt Jane warned, "Never go too close to the edge. You might fall."

Kim and her cousin Doug played in the sandbox, building roads and piling high mounds of sand for mountains. Playtime went without any incidences for about a week until Kim's homesickness became overwhelming for her.

Then, when no one was looking, Kim took off her black patent leather shoes and threw them over the fence. She stood near the edge and watched as they cascaded down the cliff. She thought, *If I'm bad, Aunt Jane will call Mom and tell her to come get me.*

But Aunt Jane didn't call Mom. Instead she told Kim, "I don't know what's gotten into you, but you can't go with Doug to play with the neighbor kids. You are on restriction."

Two weeks later Kim's parents finally arrived. Kim ran to the car and hugged them again and again. When Aunt Jane told them about the feathers and shoes incidents, Mom asked, "Kim, why did you act like that?"

Kim simply replied, "I wanted to go home."

Many years passed before Kim understood the reason for her sudden visit to the mountains. After leaving Kim there, Mom made plans to divorce her dad, but she didn't follow through. In her child's mind, Kim had sensed the mounting stress at home. In the mountains, her inability to express her fears of the unknown made her feel insecure. She craved attention and acted out. It was her childlike way of crying out for help.

Words from Jeenie

Kim acted out of a sense of great distress. She knew something was dreadfully wrong, but was not sure what it was. In my therapy office, I often deal with divorcing families. I always encourage the parents to be honest with their children, telling them as much information as is age-appropriate.

The cry for help comes in a variety of forms. Kim's cry was throwing her pretty shoes down a cliff.

Sometimes adults are so overwhelmed with unbearable desperation, rather than throwing their shoes, they stand at the edge of the proverbial cliff wondering whether anyone would care if they hurled themselves to the bottom of the gorge.

I HAVE HAD ENOUGH, LORD

Edge is described in the *Random House Dictionary of the English Language* as "a brink or verge: *the edge of a cliff; the edge of disaster.*" *On edge* implies a state of potential irritability; tenseness; nervousness; eager impatience.

Haven't we all been on the edge at one time or another? Often those struggling with depression and suicidal thoughts raise red flags by making comments like, "Life just isn't worth living anymore," or "I'm tired of living." These are cries for help.

So many times life presents the unexpected, and even as adults, we demonstrate our inner turmoil by acting out. All of us could share stories of good times turning bad—feeling we reached the pinnacle of success, only to have it suddenly snatched away.

Suddenly your view of life doesn't look so wonderful anymore. You're standing on the edge with a whirlwind of troubles swirling around you. Your pain feels like huge boulders weighting down your shoulders. You don't know what's come over you, but fear consumes your hope like a raging fire. You've isolated yourself, going without sleep and nourishment. Yet you yearn for a way out of the despair that has caused feelings of defeat and confusion. You want to run—and not look back. "Lord, just let me die."

The prophet Elijah went through such an experience. Let's take a close look at this great prophet of God. Elijah had fought against evil and won. He witnessed God's miraculous demonstration of power in opposition to worthless idols and then killed 450 prophets of Baal and 400 prophets of Asherah.

Yet when a message threatening Elijah's life arrived from wicked Queen Jezebel, his determination turned into doubts and his unrelenting faith melted into fear. This caused his heart to race and his brain to send a message to his feet that shouted, "Run." So he fled for his life, dropping from the pinnacle of success to a pit of despair.

He came to a broom tree, sat down under it and prayed that he might die. "I have had enough, Lord," he said. "Take my life; I am no better than my ancestors." Then he lay down under the tree and fell asleep.

All at once an angel touched him and said, "Get up and eat." He looked around, and there by his head was a cake of bread baked over hot coals, and a jar of water. He ate and drank and then lay down again.

The angel of the Lord came back a second time and touched him and said, "Get up and eat, for the journey is too much for you." So he got up and ate and drank. Strengthened by the food, he traveled forty days and forty nights until he reached Horeb, the mountain of God. There he went into a cave and spent the night.
—1 Kings 19:4–9

In the morning the Lord came to him and asked him to come out on the mountain and stand in His presence.

Then a great and powerful wind tore the mountains apart and shattered the rocks before the Lord, but the Lord was not in the wind. After the wind there was an earthquake, but the Lord was not in the earthquake. After the earthquake came a fire, but the Lord was not in the fire. And after the fire came a gentle whisper. When Elijah heard it, he pulled his cloak over his face and went out and stood at the mouth of the cave.
—1 Kings 19:11–13

Join Elijah on that mountain. Feel his hopelessness as you witness a great wind, an earthquake, and a consuming fire. Learn the truth as Elijah did. After he witnessed these things, a gentle voice whispered, *"What are you doing here, Elijah?"* (v. 13).

Then, in spite of his fears, Elijah once again found the courage to leave the cave and complete the work that God has given him. Embrace the truth as did Elijah.

- God will never leave you.
- God offers faith, hope, and love.
- God has a plan for your life.

In our next story a pastor describes how he struggled in a cave of despair. Des says: "I reasoned the only way I could keep going was by the grace of God. I decided to approach each new day with the aim of surviving a few hours at a time. Yet, I knew a day would dawn when I would not have the strength to go on. A voice within whispered, Why wait for that day? Why not just go ahead and end things now?"

A Ray of Light
Des Williams

As a Christian pastor, I had witnessed clinical depression. Yet, I had not been able to identify completely with the sufferer's pain. I listened, tried to understand, and was as supportive as possible. Yet, human limitations meant that I, like other pastors, could not feel another's pain and despair as intensely as the person concerned. Nothing could have prepared me for what was to happen.

The frustrations and discouragements of Christian ministry had occasionally caused bouts of the blues. Usually, those moments lasted no longer than a day. Then I'd emerge with a good night's sleep and a renewed attitude.

When the depression hit, I assumed it would pass, but this time, though, I didn't return from the pit. In fact, I sank deeper and deeper until the daylight at the top became progressively smaller. Finally, it disappeared completely. At first I felt a raw stab of pain deep inside. In those days, the pain felt so sharp that I would wince and need to control my breathing. *How weird*, I thought, *that mental illness should have such physical symptoms.*

At that time, I felt a sense of hopelessness and had a gloomy outlook on life and all it contained. I experienced a yearning to change my circumstances. I reasoned, *Maybe I should quit my pastorate and find another church. Maybe I should leave full-time ministry altogether and find a job in the secular world.*

I tried to convince myself that the antidepressants prescribed by my doctor would eventually work, but I never believed it. Spiritually, I dug my heels in and tried to trust God. I had heard and read many testimonies of Christians who had reached rock bottom and held on to God. In time they had experienced His peace. I continued to pray and read my Bible each day. I went through the motions of intimacy with God. I owed it to my congregation to have something to say from the pulpit on Sundays.

As I sunk even deeper into depression, the pain stopped. Everything stopped. In place of the pain, there was nothing— no feelings, no emotions—just emptiness and blackness. Then the thought of suicide became an option. In fact it became less of an option and more of a compulsion—a way out of the nothingness.

I yearned for death. On a train journey I fantasized about saving the train from a disaster and in doing so dying a hero. Then I'd have it all—death and being held in people's high esteem. I envied terminal cancer patients. They had an end in sight. They could prepare for death with dignity and with the support, sympathy, and understanding of those around them. No one would understand that I had a serious illness, one of the spirit and body.

My wife Susan didn't understand. And the few friends who knew about my emotional turmoil didn't understand. Comments like, "Just get over it!" didn't make sense to me and pushed me deeper into the pit. I doubted that even God understood. *I'm all alone,* I thought.

As my illness progressed, to my shame, I gave up on God. I ceased going through the pretense of a devotional life and stopped praying. At that point I decided I would die.

I set a date, 14 days away, and chose the method. It seemed like planning a trip or a dinner date. I felt calm, in control, unemotional. I thought, *This is a logical remedy, but it should look like an accident.* I had seen the effect suicide had on a person's family and friends. I could not put Susan and the kids through the heartbreak of suicide. Taking positive action felt good. Arranging my death lifted a weight from my shoulders. Bizarrely and ironically, for the first time for many weeks I felt like I had something to live for—death! I saw it as the ultimate healing.

The appointed day arrived—and went. I marveled, *I am still alive.*

What changed? I can't explain it. Somehow, by the grace of God, I perceived a ray of light that day. I tried to reason why things changed, perhaps the effects of my medication. Or a result of the counseling I had received. Maybe, the faithful love and prayers of the few people who knew of my private hell had made a difference. However, I think the change in me came from the power of Scripture a friend shared with me some weeks earlier. That promise can be found in Jeremiah 31:3–4.

"I have loved you with an everlasting love;
 I have drawn you with loving-kindness.
 I will build you up again and you will be rebuilt."

I stood on the edge, but walked away with a deeper compassion for those individuals struggling with depression. I am grateful God did not give up on me.

☼ ☼ ☼

Words from Jeenie

Clients often tell me something like this, "The depressive hole is real. I'll never be able to climb out." It is dark, overpowering, and each day they sink deeper into the mire of despair. Encouragement often does not get through to them.

I recall what happened to a Christian medical doctor whom I knew personally. One day I heard him speak to a group of therapists on depression, and he gave personal details of his lifelong struggle. I had never seen that side of him, nor had others. He was compassionate and competent, and his depression was well hidden.

Later, not unlike Pastor Williams, he carefully laid out a plan for his wife and children. Then in a rented motel room, he put a gun to his head and pulled the trigger.

Our group of professionals was shaken to the core. How could we have missed all the signs? We were trained to know, trained to respond. Yet, we were unaware…

In our next story Ashima spiraled into a depression after the death of her father. She reasoned that she'd do anything to end the pain—even take her own life.

Make the Pain Go Away
Ashima Arora

My mind screamed, *Make the pain go away. My heart hurts too much.*

Shivering, I reached for the sweatshirt lying on the backseat and slipped it on. The sun had set hours before. My car sat at the far end of the train station parking lot, several yards from the tracks. *If I glimpse the glare of a train's lights in the distance, it would only take a few seconds to drive my car into the train's path,* I reasoned.

How did I end up here?

I looked around at the empty food wrappers and bags strewn on the car's seat and floor. I had spent the afternoon and evening driving aimlessly, stopping to buy food and eat. Overeat is probably more accurate. My stomach hurt and my head throbbed from lack of sleep. Sadness, guilt, anger, fear, shame, and exhaustion filled my mind, heart, and soul.

I gripped the steering wheel and fought to hold back the tears that threatened to overflow.

Why do I feel this way?

Dad had died a few months earlier. Yet, I could barely think about it, let alone talk about his illness and the pain I felt watching him take his final breath. The past few months were a blur of closing Dad's finances, paying bills, and sorting through his belongings. Now everything was finished, and I had nothing to do except feel stuck alone in a valley of grief.

Do I really want to die?

Part of me knew this was not the solution to my grief. I desired to forget everything and not feel anything. Truthfully, I was scared—afraid the despair deep inside would never leave. Scared to admit I was considering ending my life, rather than running to God for help and comfort. *I don't deserve to call myself a Christian. I know God does not want me to kill myself. But, I'm hurting too much inside to pray. Is there anyone out there who cares?*

Everybody else had moved on with his or her lives, and I wasn't sure anyone wanted to listen to me. Still, I pulled out my cell phone from my purse and flipped through the list of names. *Who should I call? I really want to call Lisa. We've always been able to talk. But she's been too busy since she had the baby. Samantha? She's usually asleep by now. I'll send her a text message. If she's sleeping, the text won't wake her up. But what if she's not there?*

I sent the message, and immediately the phone buzzed with Samantha's reply. I texted her back and said, "I'll call you in a few minutes." I drove home, weary and frightened. Once there, I called Samantha and told her about the anguish I felt inside.

She listened and said, "Ashima, I really care about you. Don't ever doubt that I care."

I wanted to tell her what I tried to do, but the words stuck inside my throat. For now it was enough to know someone was willing to listen. Someone cared. The conversation ended, and I tried to sleep.

I wondered, *What stopped me from ending my life tonight?*

The answer came in a still, quiet voice, *God stopped you.*
He pulled you away from the line you wanted to cross. He made Samantha
available so you could talk. He has been speaking to you throughout all of this.
He wants you to experience contentment and peace, not this intense turmoil of
emotions. In the midst of this valley of grief, there is light.

Finally I was able to pray. "Lord, I'm overwhelmed. I hardly
have words to express my thoughts. Please give me the strength
to face my actions and emotions and the courage to be honest
about my intentions tonight. Lord, I need help. I can't cope
with this grief on my own. I'm ready to take a step to climb out
of the valley. Lord, please lead the way."

And He did.

In my alarm I said,
"I am cut off from your sight!"
Yet you heard my cry for mercy
when I called to you for help.
—Psalm 31:22

☀ ☀ ☀

Words from Jeenie

Numerous times I've dealt with suicidal ideation in therapy.
Not only does the patient feel helpless, but so does the
counselor. I've shot up prayers during sessions, "O, God, I
don't know what more to say. Give me Your wisdom to reach
out to this dear soul with Your words, love, and comfort."

My desire is that they have an additional confidant to
call (besides me) when the feelings of suicide overwhelm
them. We sign a "No Suicide" contract with various
stipulations. Sometimes I talk until I'm blue in the face,
hoping something will connect. Then, I must trust God to
keep them safe in His care.

Sadly, sometimes a person goes over the edge as shown in the following poem.

THE UNCLE I NEVER KNEW
Charles R. Brown

He was one of five brothers,
Born in 1915, second oldest after Dad.
He died in the service.
That's what I was told.
He was 31.
I was about 2,
so there's only vague memories
in my childhood
of a soldier in uniform
framed on the wall of my
grandparents' home.
It was one of those fuzzy memories
of a yellowed, brown and white photograph.
There were no stories of his youth.
No recollections of youthful pranks—
Only the picture.
And that he had died in the service.
I knew the other uncles;
some better than others.
Dad and those three shared
a characteristic "sunshine" smile
that seemed to say,
"Hey, come sit by me."
But this one… I never knew.
All I had ever been told was that
he died in the service.
Some were told he died of cancer.
Later I was told, "Yes, he did

die in the service."
He was found under a tree,
his lifeblood drained from his body
from self-inflicted cuts to his wrists.
I didn't know him.
I wish I had.
I hope he was ready
—this uncle I never knew.

—

Not understanding the urge that called out to Jana to end her life, she found herself standing on the rooftop of an abandoned building. She felt empty like the rooms under her feet. So she stood on the edge in a life-and-death struggle.

Close to the Edge
Jana Ray

I walked over to answer the phone, feeling numb inside.
"Hello," I said listlessly.
    "Mom, is that you?" my son Kent asked.
    "Yes, of course it's me," I snapped.
    "I'm at Dad's, and I need you to watch Eric for the day."
    "OK, I guess so."
    "Great! We'll be over in a couple of hours."
    I hung up without saying goodbye. An image of my
18-month-old grandson flashed in my mind. I thought,
I love my grandson, but I should have told Kent no.
    "I'm too tired." I whispered, "No sleep makes a woman
dull and rude. Why can't I find joy and fulfillment in my life?"
I wiped the tears away and sat down next to the phone. "I have
to call Kent back and tell him I can't watch Eric. I just can't!"
    The phone rang and rang. Finally I heard Kent's voice,
"Howdy!"

"Kent, this is Mom. I . . . I'm sorry but something has come up, and I can't watch the baby."

"Are you all right, Mom?"

"Yes, I just have some urgent business."

"OK. I'll call you later to see how you're doing."

After hanging up, I sat there feeling worse than before. My kids would be better off without me. I felt darkness closing in—the overpowering blackness of depression. I no longer could stand to go through the motions of living. When even the joy of a new grandchild could not penetrate the dark clouds, I realized that hopelessness dominated my every breath.

A voice within whispered, *Hang in there a little longer. Tomorrow may be better. Tomorrow you lead the music in church. Tomorrow maybe joy will return.* I decided to suffer through one more night.

Sunday brought the sunshine, and somewhere beyond the black fog that had invaded my mind, I heard birds singing. Then the darkness again completely engulfed me, shutting everything else out.

"I am sick, sick of living!" I screamed. I dressed quickly not caring what I wore or what I looked like. I got into my car and drove to the cemetery. I sat at my mother's grave and cried until uncontrollable sobs shook my whole body. It had been two years since Mom had passed away.

As I got back into my car, a strange resolve—almost a calmness—overtook me. I knew what I wanted to do. I drove to an unoccupied building complex that I'd driven by for weeks. I parked my car and went around to the back where I climbed a ladder to the rooftop. When I got to the top, I looked down at the hard, cold concrete below. I thought, *With my luck I will end up crippled, not dead.*

A still voice whispered, "Ask for help."

"Help! I do need help, God. I do need help. Please take this darkness away." After I prayed, I found a new strength— one that helped me turn away from the ledge of that roof.

I left the rooftop and ventured back into the world where I sought the counsel of a psychiatrist. He diagnosed me as manic depressive or bipolar. Medication treated my disorder and leveled out my mood swings.

I pray that by reading my story, others will realize that there is light at the end of the tunnel. God looks at each of us and understands our individual pain. He'll help you reach out to friends, family, or professionals just as He did for me.

☀ ☀ ☀

Words from Jeenie

I am a firm believer that we serve a miracle-working Lord—One who can instantly or progressively heal all types of illness if He chooses. Having said that, in my practice I have seen God's help for mental illness come through medication in many cases. God often uses the help of a psychiatrist who prescribes therapeutic drugs to alleviate or correct a physiological problem.

I am not a believer in long-term medication if it's not necessary. However, I believe there are some disorders that require lifelong treatment. As a therapist, I think a believer needs to look for a Christian counselor when seeking treatment. Often the counselor can refer the client to a competent psychiatrist, hopefully also a Christian.

REFLECTIONS

1. Take your fears to the Lord. Write them down. Then mentally hand them to Him.

2. Describe how God has renewed your spirit.

Prayer

Lord, I trust You to take the despair away. Help me to remember that I am not alone. You are with me. Nourish my soul and fill me with Your Word. In Jesus's name I pray, amen.

CHAPTER 9

SAVING A LIFE

Heal me, O Lord, and I will be healed;
save me and I will be saved,
for you are the one I praise.
—Jeremiah 17:14

Remember the song, "Count Your Blessings"? From the first breath we take, life in itself is a gift. Among the many amazing features of our bodies are our five senses: sight, hearing, taste, smell, and touch. It is with these senses we are able to embrace the world around us: wiggle our toes in the sand at the beach, smell pine trees on a mountain trail, view the beauty of a rainbow after a rainstorm. Our taste buds allow us to savor the flavor of our favorite foods, and we can enjoy holding the hand of someone we love. These are a few of the blessings in life.

Most people are able to endure the valleys of life long enough to reach the next peak. Through Christ, the believer has the strength and ability to not just survive but overcome many challenges. Yet for some, a time comes when all strength seems gone. For instance, the illness of depression can leave a person feeling isolated, lonely, and hopeless. When people are clinically depressed, they don't necessarily want to die. Instead their actions often act as a plea for help.

Those who have attempted suicide commonly face daily the need for medication, counseling, and in some cases, the fear that depression might win out over their desire to live. There are times when intervention from a friend or family member makes a difference and saves a life.

Let's compare two scenarios.

A. After a terrible car accident, injuries placed Jenny in the hospital. Her doctor explained, "You'll have to take it easy for a while. You have a concussion, broken leg, and bruised ribs."

Jenny wondered, *Who's going to take care of my kids?*

Visits from family and friends brought encouragement and answers to her problems. Her friend Bonnie said, "I'll watch the kids for you."

A mechanic who was a church member said, "I heard that your car is totaled. I think I've found a good replacement for you."

In time, Jenny healed both physically and emotionally.

B. Carol is a woman struggling with clinical depression. Friends and family members didn't understand her illness and often said things like, "Get on with your life. Stop moping around all the time. You aren't any fun to be with anymore." Carol felt ashamed so she didn't seek professional help.

One afternoon Carol came home and found a note from her husband, saying, "I need to get away from here for a while." She walked into her bathroom and pulled a bottle of pills out of the medicine cabinet. She popped a handful in her mouth. She did not stop to reason as she swallowed a second handful. Then she lay down on her bed.

Fortunately, her teenage daughter came upstairs shortly thereafter. "Mom, wake up!" Lisa cried, shaking her. When there was no response, she dialed 911.

Carol's family doctor suggested counseling, and her husband agreed to go along.

The incident acted as a wake-up call to Carol, as well as to her friends and family. Through therapy and medication, Carol's life improved. Her husband and friends finally realized that she had an illness, and they rallied to help.

There needs to be a deeper acceptance and understanding that depression is an illness—one that is treatable. When a person is in an accident, his injuries are visible and are treated with skillful hands and sympathetic words. Depression and other mental illnesses need to be treated with the same compassion.

One morning at work, Lynne felt a sudden urge to check on her sister.

One More Day to Live
Lynne Michaels

My day began with its usual frenzied activity as I got my children off to school and drove to my office. Once there, I poured a cup of coffee, then sat down at my desk and began dictating a letter to my secretary. Midway through the letter, my mind wandered. I paused and fought to regain my concentration.

"Lynne, is everything OK?" my secretary asked.

Setting down my coffee cup, I said a silent prayer. *God, I've got this feeling that things are not OK with my sister. Should I go to her house? Should I go now?*

"Lynne? Is something wrong?"

The feeling became stronger. Immediately I stood up and grabbed my purse. "Vicki, I've got to leave. I'll be back, but I have to check on my sister."

With my heart pounding, I raced to my car. Driving those five miles to Shannon's home seemed like forever. Once there, I rang the doorbell. Then without waiting for an answer, I scrambled for my keys and opened her door. I called out, "Shannon, it's Lynne. Are you home?"

No answer brought dread to my heart. I ran through the house and even opened the shower door in case...

"Shannon, where are you?" I screamed.

God, You've got to help me. Where is she?

I turned and looked through the sliding glass door. I saw Shannon lying in a lounge chair. Quickly, I pushed the sliding glass door open and knelt beside her.

"Shannon, talk to me, just talk to me."

She moaned.

"Thank You, God. She's alive!" Immediately I phoned the paramedics.

The following week I sat by Shannon's hospital bed, watched her heart monitor, and listened to the steady beat.

God, thank You. Thank You for that still small voice that told me to go check on my sister.

In silence, I brushed Shannon's hair away from her eyes. I felt helpless as I knew that I could not brush away the despair and confusion of Shannon's mental illness. I knew that life was ultimately her choice and one that I could not make for her.

Thank You, God, I prayed. *Thanks for today, a day to live, a day that I have to love my sister.*

☀ ☀ ☀

God often speaks to us in a quiet, yet rather nagging way. When that happens, it is imperative that we listen and take action, as did Lynne.

One day Jeenie received a phone call from a client that required immediate action.

"Why I Called You"
Jeenie Gordon

One Saturday, a client, who had received my private number through a speaking brochure, telephoned my home. My heart pounded as she softly slurred out her words. "Jeenie, I took a bottle of meds."

I questioned what they were, but she didn't know. Since I was not in my office, I did not remember the medication she was taking, nor her address. Over and over I asked, "Tell me your address." Hesitantly she finally mumbled it.

Immediately I called her psychiatrist on his emergency cell phone. He remembered what medication she was taking and stated, "An overdose can kill her."

Dialing 911, I was able to give her location. "We're on the way," the paramedics assured me. Later, I was able to locate her husband.

The next week she came in for a therapy session to continue dealing with her underlying issues. "I didn't really want to die, Jeenie. That's why I called you."

I knew God had led my client to reach out to me in her time of desperation. We continued in therapy for another year, and I saw great improvement and emotional health emerge. The suicidal thinking ceased.

※ ※ ※

Who Is My Neighbor?

We find a powerful lesson in Luke 10:25–37. A man of the law approached Jesus and asked Him a question, mainly to test His knowledge. *"Teacher," he asked, "what must I do to inherit eternal life?"* (v. 25). Perhaps the man had a smug look on his face as he tried to trap Jesus. Jesus answered with a question in return.

> *"What is written in the Law?" he replied. "How do you read it?"*
> *He answered: "Love the Lord your God with all your heart and with all your soul and with all your strength and with all your mind"; and, "Love your neighbor as yourself."*
> —Luke 10:26–27

Jesus told the man he had answered correctly, but the man wanted to justify himself, so he asked Jesus to explain whom his neighbor was.

In reply Jesus said: "A man was going down from Jerusalem to Jericho, when he fell into the hands of robbers. They stripped him of his clothes, beat him and went away, leaving him half dead. A priest happened to be going down the same road, and when he saw the man, he passed by on the other side. So too, a Levite, when he came to the place and saw him, passed by on the other side. But a Samaritan, as he traveled, came where the man was; and when he saw him, he took pity on him. He went to him and bandaged his wounds, pouring on oil and wine. Then he put the man on his own donkey, took him to an inn and took care of him.

"Which of these three do you think was a neighbor to the man who fell into the hands of robbers?

The expert in the law replied, "The one who had mercy on him." Jesus told him, "Go and do likewise"
—Luke 10:30–34, 36–37

The good Samaritan is a parable that is as profound today as it was in the time of Christ—because it points to the very essence of love and mercy. Do you think that man left with a deeper understanding of God's heart? Isn't God saying the same thing to us?

If you know someone who is struggling with depression, do you walk away ignoring their cries for help? Or do you offer words of encouragement, or help them in some other way? You can help by giving your time, listening to them, and answering their questions. You can cook a meal for them or direct them to a professional.

In our next story Karen discovered a deeper meaning for her journey to the emergency room as a patient. She left the hospital, not only feeling physically better, but with a profound awe for God's sovereignty.

God's Emergency Room
Karen Kosman

I awoke early one morning with heart arrhythmias. *Not again,* I thought. Having suffered with this condition for years, I found myself slipping into thoughts of self-pity. *Why me? I've had enough.*

Then self-justification for my pity party followed. *Don't be so hard on yourself. It's natural to feel this way under these conditions.* But then in a surreal moment came the realization, *I need to go to the hospital!*

I reached over and woke my husband, "John, I'm in a-fib. You need to drive me to the hospital."

"OK, let's go." We both dressed quickly and were soon on our way.

A short time later, I found myself flat on my back on a gurney, staring up at the ceiling in the ER. I'd grown accustomed to being hooked up to an IV, a heart monitor, and oxygen tubes.

Before another cycle of self-pity hit, I heard my doctor talking to the man in the next cubicle. "Sam, wake up. Have you been depressed? I need to know what you took."

Quickly my focus changed from poor me to poor man. *God, please be with Sam,* I prayed silently.

I knew all too well the devastation of suicide. I'd lost a son to suicide. God had carried me through difficult times and had brought compassion into my heart for those struggling with depression.

Moments later Dr. Ervin stood by my bedside.

"Karen, your heart rate has slowed, but you are still in a-fib. We're going to move you across the hall to another section of the ER. You'll be more comfortable there."

"OK," I replied. I looked at John and sighed. "I was hoping we could go home."

With my husband by my side, I was rolled through two large doors and down the hallway into the next section. Moving from the gurney to the bed while tubes tangled from my body wasn't easy.

A nurse assisted me. "Hi. My name is Jill." Something shimmering around her neck caught my eye—a cross. Her brown eyes sparkled as she said, "You're going to be OK."

"I know." I answered, staring at her cross.

Turning to my husband, I smiled and said, "John, I feel comfortable, knowing my nurse probably is a Christian."

Looking over at Jill, he said, "Karen is an author. She has to finish the book she is working on."

Jill squeezed my hand and said, "So we need to get you well. Do you write fiction?"

"No. I write nonfiction, dealing with real-life issues."

With tears in her eyes Jill said, "I've been sober for seven years, but I'm separated from my husband. I hope he'll give up his drinking and come home."

For the next several minutes I shared with Jill about the multiple traumas I'd overcome. I told her how I'd met John and the wholeness we both found in our faith.

A short time later I heard Jill tell another nurse, "She's going to be OK. God sent her here for a purpose, besides encouraging me."

I knew they were talking about me because I was the only patient on that side of the ER. I smiled. *I'm the one who received encouragement from Jill.* Again I thought about Sam and prayed, *Lord, please help Sam. Help him to know You have a plan for his life.*

A whooshing noise erupted as the doors opened, and a gurney appeared. I recognized the patient as the man who had been next to me in the other section. Again, the nurse and doctor asked Sam questions. I watched, listened, and prayed.

The doctor moved away from Sam's side and walked over to the nurse's station where he studied the monitors. Then I heard him say, "Looks like her heart rate is normal." Moments later he stood by my bed and said, "If you're not something! You just converted back."

"You mean I can go home?"

"Yes."

Jill walked in smiling and said, "I knew you'd be OK."

"Thank you for all your help. May I speak with Sam?"

"OK, but officially I don't know about this," Jill replied as she unhooked my monitors and IV.

I got dressed and walked to the other side of the room, closing the curtain behind me. I found Sam still unconscious, but I trusted that he'd hear me.

"Sam, I'm not a nurse, I'm a patient, too. I wanted you to know that you are going to be OK. I know the heartache of depression, and I lost a son to suicide. I'll be praying for you. God has a great plan for your life if you choose to live."

His hand moved, although his eyes didn't open. The next thing I knew his hand lay in mine. I smiled because I knew he'd heard me. His eyes fluttered but remained shut.

What a strange day, I thought. *Who'd have guessed that a trip to the ER could be so full of promise and encouragement?*

Suddenly, I remembered my question upon waking with an irregular heartbeat. *Why me?* And I realized that my question had been answered through the thoughtfulness of a nurse who shared a part of herself with me and a man named Sam who needed someone to care.

Thank You, God, for giving me a glimpse into Your emergency room.

☀ ☀ ☀

Words from Jeenie

Karen listened to the still, small voice of God urging her to speak with Sam. Often we feel embarrassed to follow God's prompting. *They'll think I'm intruding. What if it does no good? What if the hospital staff is angry and throws me out?*

I suspect Karen did not question herself, but quickly acted according to God's direction. We will probably never know until we reach heaven the extent to which God has used us when we choose to obey. May there be more compassionate people like Karen.

The parents of a 15-year-old girl loved their daughter enough to seek help, although it was painful to leave her in a mental hospital. They helped their daughter, and now she wants to help others.

Breaking Point
Kallie

"I am barely 15, and I am in a mental hospital," I cried. "I can't live like this anymore. What has happened to me?" I glanced around my hospital room at the bare, white walls and thought, *This place resembles my life.*

Unable to bear the pain, I collapsed on the cold tile floor, my body convulsing with sobs.

Thoughts of the past swirled in my mind. My friends had told lies about me—lies that evolved into "truths" in my own head. Dreams of dying persisted, starting at the age of 11. The potent addiction of burning, banging, scratching, picking, and cutting my body every day for the past 18 months caused me to feel alive.

"That's all I want," I cried, "to feel alive, to get rid of the numbness that has haunted me for so long. I want this despair, this insomnia, this perpetual exhaustion, these thoughts, this hideous restlessness to stop. I want it all to stop!"

A sinister, familiar voice in my mind taunted me again. *That's the reason you act like such an idiot, Kallie. I can't believe you. Look at what you do to your family and friends. Remember the time you took those pills, trying to kill yourself? You almost succeeded, but you failed. Instead, you ended up in the hospital, drinking thick black charcoal. That charcoal resembles the color of your soul—black with no sign of change.*

I wanted the voice to stop, but it continued, *Remember, Kallie, those boyfriends who took control of you? How about the night you took three times the amount of pills that would normally kill someone? What now, Kallie? You screamed at the friends who only wanted to save your life. Yes, you can acquire freedom from this hospital, but if you do, you'll resume the haunting addictions.*

"I can't change. The doctors tell me I will permanently live this way. A vicious cycle possesses me and will encompass my life forever."

Suddenly a new, calmer voice floated across my mind. *Kallie, you've tried everything this world has to offer in attempt to stop this pain. Those endeavors did not alleviate anything. Your parents have always said that God will remove all of this pain you possess. Why not give Him a chance?*

"What has God done for me? Why has He let me feel this way? Besides, I don't believe He even exists. People with wishful dreams fabricated Him ages ago."

Suddenly, something inside of me began to change. *Perhaps God does exist. Perhaps He can help me.* I cried out, "O God, I need help so desperately. Please, transform me. I can't do this anymore. I can't live another day in this hell. Help me find Kallie, the girl who had good grades, played in sports, and worked on the student council. Just take this numbness away and let me feel alive again! Please, God, I just want to feel alive."

I will always remember that night as the night my life was transformed. For years, I chose society's lies and found malevolent thoughts roaming my mind until that one surreal moment when everything changed. It happened on the worst night of my life; it became the best night of my life.

I called to God for help, and He heard me. That night in the hospital my world changed, and my new life began. God resurrected me, and now I feel alive! I am filled with joy, and my smile is real instead of a pasted-on grin to please society. For the first time, I wake up with an inconceivable excitement at the opportunity to live another day rather than dreading the thought of even waking up.

I have learned in weak moments when my heart tries to play tug-of-war and Satan's taunting lies return, I don't have to listen. I don't fear regressing because God loves me with such a magnitude that I am set free.

I love others with a passion and believe God healed me so I can help the next generation. For I am living proof that a person can overcome even when society labels him or her as doomed.

Numerous teens unnecessarily wander from hospital to hospital, pill to pill, razor to razor, attempt to attempt, boy to boy. My message to them is, "Every word that slices your heart, every demon that rages in your head, every need for the blood to roll down your wrist can be rendered powerless because God furnishes something tremendous. He is able to resuscitate broken souls and create wholeness. His love is not a temporary high but resides permanently inside you."

My desire is to work in a home for teens and help them discover release from their carousels of pain and addiction. A life worth living awaits, and I want to share it with each and every one of those empty hearts who are approaching their last chance in life. This generation can receive restoration—the crimson tears can stop—but only with the love and the life that Christ provides.

☼ ☼ ☼

Words from Jeenie

Kallie was similar to scores of teens I've counseled at the high-school level. Even though her drug and cutting addictions greatly complicated the situation, the underlying issue was enormous pain and her reaction to it, which Kallie had not addressed. Yet, in time, Kallie cried to God for help, which is the best thing she could have done.

Most teens do not have the ability to look deeply within themselves and decide to make changes. First, they do not know what to do and, second, they are unable to do it alone. They need professional help

Often family and friends are clueless regarding clinical interventions. Therefore, a professional needs to be involved. Even then, it undoubtedly will be a long, hard struggle to conquer an addiction.

During recovery, God also provides caring people, such as a therapist, counselor, support group, or church group to help a person become emotionally healthy. And, at the end of the road, there is hope.

─── ❧ ───

FROM DARKNESS TO LIGHT
C.A.N.

I've been on a roller-coaster ride
Between life and death.

I lost my faith;
I lost my hope;
I lost my way;
I could no longer cope.

I cried out in pain,
Longing to be heard and understood.
If someone didn't intervene,
I wouldn't be around much longer.

I was slipping fast,
Unable to go on,
Falling deeper and deeper.
What was the point of holding on?

I searched for a reason
To keep fighting for my life.
Obstacles knocked me down.
I no longer had the strength to get back up.

God spoke to me
When I was at the end of my rope,

Giving me a reason to go on
And the ability to cope.
Death was no longer an option.
My focus became life.
The pieces of the puzzle
Began to fall into place.

———

Jeenie will never forget the day Anthony stumbled into her high school counseling office.

"Remember Me?"

Jeenie Gordon

He slammed the door, making the windows shake. Then he collapsed in the chair beside my desk. Desperately he pounded his fists on my desk, cursing and yelling. All the while, tears splashed down his shirt.

Silently I waited.

Slowly he began to open up. His parents had split up, just before his high school graduation. What should have been the most exciting day of his life, he anticipated with gut-wrenching pain.

For two hours we talked.

As he was leaving, he commented, "I want you to know, Mrs. Gordon, that as I passed by your office window at lunchtime, I knew I had to talk to you. Actually, I was on my way home to blow out my brains."

Three years later, with a bright smile on his face, Anthony once again stood in my doorway. "Hey, there, remember me?"

I smiled and nodded.

In tow was an adorable, blonde, blue-eyed two-year-old girl. Setting her on his knee, he stated. "This is my little daughter. I'm now married and an electrician's apprentice. Life is good."

We had a long chat, catching up on his life. He gave me a hug as they left.

With tears glistening in my eyes, I thought, *If I had not been there for him, he would have missed all this. Thank You, heavenly Father, for using me.*

A life was saved.

≋ ≋ ≋

Reflections

1. Describe some ways you can help a neighbor.

2. Describe positive ways to show love toward a suicidal or mentally ill person.

Prayer

Lord, You have taught me how precious life is. Help me to reach out to the brokenhearted. Bring them closer to You through my compassion. Let Your light shine through me. In Jesus's name I pray, amen.

CHAPTER 10

FORGIVENESS: THE PATH TO FREEDOM

"And when you stand praying, if you hold anything against anyone, forgive him, so that your Father in heaven may forgive you your sins."
—Mark 11:25

Unforgiveness traps the heart, mind, and soul in an unrelenting cycle of grief. It touches the lives of both the young and old—a jailer of those who desperately need to be set free. It comes in many forms: regret, sorrow, hopelessness, revenge, and self-blame. Standing guard over unforgiving thoughts is anger, whose accusing taunts torment the mind.

People whose hearts are unforgiving travel a road of grief. They remain guarded and silent as they try desperately to find peace. Messages woven in lies often play in their minds. *You don't deserve to be forgiven. How can God forgive you? How can you possibly forgive that person? It's too late!* And often thoughts of revenge steal contentment. No one is immune from being trapped by bitterness and unforgiveness.

In this chapter we touch on different issues surrounding forgiveness that accompany suicide or attempted suicide.

In the following story a man, struggling with his attempted suicide, turns to Dr. Downing for help.

Embracing Truth

Dr. Kevin Downing

A man, I'll call him Jeff, who had been a patient in a local
ER, came to see me for counseling. Single and in his late 30s,
he'd been a successful businessman. Intelligent and gifted, he
struggled with pride and a spirit of superiority. Full of grief,
he felt his suicide attempt had done irreparable damage to his
reputation. In counseling he presented me with some of his
entrenched beliefs.

"I can never own up to or explain why I attempted suicide,"
said Jeff.

"You already are owning up to what you did by talking with
another person about what happened," I replied. "Sharing what
happened is the first step, and to do so in counseling is even
better. You don't owe everyone an explanation, and at some
level, there is no complete explanation. It was what it was.

"There are a multitude of factors that can lead a person to
try to take his or her life. These elements are for you and maybe
a very small circle of people to know, not the evening news.
Smart, honest friends know about the feelings of hopelessness
and despair that come with suicide attempts because they have
all been there. No, not everyone acts on these feelings, but nearly
everyone has these feelings at some time in their life."

He sat there a moment, then added, "OK, but too many
people know about my attempt. I feel I have to cover it up, but
I don't know how."

"Jeff, in your situation you are not going to be able to cover
it up—and you don't need to. The numbers of people who
know about it are few compared to the number of people you
are going to meet and rub shoulders with. You will make new
friends and move into new circles," I said. Then I paused.

When he didn't say anything, I continued, "As your healing
progresses, you might find that you will make your suicide
attempt part of your life story. It really is an incredible story
that at one time you wanted to take your life and now you are

in a far better place. It is a testimony of the grace of God in your life. It might become a tool to help other people. You have survived this dark night of the soul, and since you did, others just might be able too. You can decide about these things later. For now you need to heal and spend time with safe people you trust. What to do and whom to share this information with will come in time."

"I hear what you are saying, Dr. Downing, but I can never forgive myself for what I did," Jeff said. "The guilt and shame I feel is something that I just can't shake."

I responded: "I want you to imagine yourself dragging around a giant ball of guilt and shame. Imagine that your burden is so heavy that you give in to exhaustion. But you are not alone. Your friends and God Himself show up and lift the burden. Together they carry it to the foot of the Cross. And there at its base, a powerful cleansing flow begins to melt away this weight of shame and self-condemnation."

I paused and waited for Jeff's reaction. When he didn't respond, I continued, "There is only one place for guilt, and that is at the foot of the Cross. We cannot forget, and that is why we need forgiveness. Neurotic guilt points the finger of condemnation and demands us to do the impossible, to go back in time and undo something we did—something we regret. We have no time machine. This condemnation will not be satisfied with self-hatred or self-contempt. Healthy guilt, or conviction by the Holy Spirit, also prompts us to take action. However, it is action that is possible—action like apologizing for wronging another or returning something that doesn't belong to you."

Then I challenged him, "If you really hate what you did, then hate the self-condemnation that could drive you back to another suicidal depression. Propose in your heart to hate so much what you did that you will not allow yourself to harbor the seeds of self-hate that could force you back to that same place."

"Dr. Downing, there is nothing good about this."

"Actually there is something very good that has come from this. From this day forward, you will be a grace-filled, nonjudgmental person. You will never prescribe trite and simplistic solutions to the complex and painful situations that people encounter. You won't throw rocks. You have been humbled and will act humbly with others. The problem you once had with arrogance has been permanently resolved. The world needs more humble people like you. Your gift has come with a very high price that few are willing to pay. Now is the time to treasure it."

"I ruined my life by trying to kill myself," he persisted.

"Black-and-white statements are rarely true. This one is definitely not true. Your life is not ruined. You survived. Victorious songs are filled with many verses of nearly giving up—but you haven't."

I concluded with, "Like so many of us who face loss, we need to learn to live with what we do have and not live in the memory of what was or what could've or should've been. I know this is easier said than done, but I also know you can do it!"

Although Jeff is still a high achiever, he now understands he needs to be careful. He has learned not to take his depression lightly and to take better care of himself. He changed his routine to include physical exercise, a men's accountability group, prayer, reading the Bible, and periodic counseling.

Over time he embraced God's grace. Jeff forgave himself and found the ability to share and encourage others with his story.

☀ ☀ ☀

In this story Dr. Balodis was able to help a heartbroken mother who wondered if she'd ever feel whole again.

The Puzzle Pieces
Dr. Jacqueline Balodis

The phone rang, and a hysterical voice on the other end cried, "I just found out that my son shot himself. How could God let him die?"

It took me a moment to pull my thoughts together to respond to her. Then I replied, "I'm so sorry. Brenda, why don't you tell me exactly what happened?"

She took a deep breath. "My son was going to college and living with his grandmother in Illinois. I just received a call from Grandma. She had just returned home from a shopping trip. When she opened the door, her grandson's golden retriever met her. The dog was shaking all over and looked distressed. Grandma knew something was terribly wrong and started walking through the house. When she reached Jim's room, she saw him stretched out on his bed with a gun still gripped in his hand."

Brenda started sobbing again. "I should have been a better mother. I shouldn't have let him go to Illinois. He should have stayed in California with me. Where did I go wrong?"

"Brenda, I'm through seeing patients for the day, so why don't I come over. I'll be there in half an hour."

I knew Brenda blamed herself for her son's death. She also blamed God for letting it happen. On the drive over to her house, I prayed and searched for the right words to give this hurting mother.

Brenda greeted me at the door, and I hugged her, holding her in my arms for several minutes. We went into the living room and sat on the couch. I held her hand, and we were silent for several minutes. I realized my presence was what she needed more than anything.

Finally she spoke. "Why did he do this to me? Didn't he know I loved him?"

I realized at this point that Brenda blamed her son as well as herself and God. I knew it was going to take a long time for her to work through the pain. Brenda came to my office twice a week for seven months.

Sometimes I let her pour out her feelings. Other times we sat in silence. Often there is strength in quiet solitude. Every session I gave her homework as we worked on various issues she needed to deal with. That way she could progress at her own speed. Ultimately I had her write a goodbye letter to Jim.

I could see that this was the beginning of her learning to forgive herself. The letter was filled with her good memories of special times she and Jim had shared together. The more she wrote, the more her love was strengthened for Jim and the more she grew herself—loving unconditionally, dealing with and erasing "what ifs," and forgiving Jim.

During one session Brenda announced, "I understand now that Jim's death is not my fault. I couldn't have prevented it. More important, I don't blame God anymore either."

Finally, all the pieces of the puzzle came together. Once she forgave herself, her son, and God, her faith was again strengthened.

※ ※ ※

Words from Jeenie

I see four stages in forgiveness.

- *Stage One*: Admission of pain. Often, around others, we pretend that the pain isn't all that bad. We say we're doing well. Admitting the enormity of the anguish to oneself and to others is vital.
- *Stage Two*: Anger. We have a reason to be angry. Although anger is a valid emotion, it can be either constructive or destructive. A passive person may internalize fury and pretend it is not there. Another person may explode on everyone around them and about everything. Both ways are unhealthy. It is important to acknowledge and deal with our anger—but we must not get stuck in it.

- *Stage Three*: Confrontation. Even though the loved one is no longer living, there is a need to confront. A healthy way is to write an honest letter, telling the person about our anger and the pain we feel over what he or she has chosen to do.

We must also forgive ourselves. No one is perfect, and everyone could have done better. We cannot blame ourselves for a suicide. Forgiving ourselves is a must for our eventual healing.

- *Stage Four*: Forgiveness. The journey toward forgiveness is long and difficult, but the road must be traveled. It is the pathway toward wholeness. Eventually, we must forgive the suicide or attempted suicide.

Forgiveness liberates us. I believe this is why God commands it—for our freedom.

— ❦ —

PAMELA
Gary Sumner

The sudden loss of one I loved
Brought shock at first—she can't be gone.
There must be some mistake!

The minutes, hours, days that passed
Were blurred by numbing grief and loss,
The details lost to time.

My mind shut down; I could not hear
The words of comfort friends would speak
To pull me out of pain.

I spoke of Pam and who she was.
I questioned why she took her life
And what I could have done.

She could have called and talked to me.
She did before 'bout many things,
But never gave a hint…

So anger came, it overwhelmed.
I wanted so to scream at her
For such a selfish act.

Through time and prayer, forgiveness came.
Yet oft my heart will ache and cry,
I want my sister back.

<hr>

EXPERIENCE FORGIVENESS

In John 8:1–11 we read a story about a woman who faced rejection and certain death until Jesus asked a question that changed her life and her accusers' minds. As you read this story, pretend you are standing in the temple courts and let Him speak to your heart.

> *But Jesus went to the Mount of Olives. At dawn he appeared again in the temple courts, where all the people gathered around him, and he sat down to teach them.*
> —John 8:1–2

Visualize the peaceful scene of Jesus teaching those who gathered around to hear His words of hope. Then the unexpected happened as a low murmur among the crowd turned to shouts of indignation. "They caught her in adultery! Stone her."

> *They made her stand before the group and said to Jesus, "Teacher, this woman was caught in the act of adultery. In the Law Moses commanded we*

stone such women. Now what do you say?" They were using this question
as a trap, in order to have a basis for accusing him.
    But Jesus bent down and started to write on the ground with
his finger.
—John 8:3–6

A hush fell across the temple courts as they waited for His response. The woman stood helplessly looking at the surrounding crowd, her heart raging with fear. She'd surely die for her indiscretion.

The teachers of the law and the Pharisees pushed her to the center of the angry crowd. As she looked into the eyes of those holding stones she found no mercy.

Use your imagination and visualize yourself standing in the crowd. Feel the weight of a stone in your hand and the urging of your impatient heart. Your hand tightens its grip on the stone while you wait to hear the Teacher's response.

When they kept on questioning him, he straightened up and said to them,
"If any one of you is without sin, let him be the first to throw a stone at her."
Again he stooped down and wrote on the ground.
—John 8:7–8

At the impact of His words, "without sin," your grip loosens. Suddenly the rock feels heavy, and your arm aches. *Drop it,* your mind screams. There is a sense of relief as you open your hand, and the stone falls to the ground.

At this, those who heard began to go away one at a time, the older ones
first, until only Jesus was left, with the woman still standing there. Jesus
straightened up and asked her, "Woman, where are they? Has no one
condemned you?"
    "No one, sir," she said.
    "Then neither do I condemn you," Jesus declared. "Go now and leave
your life of sin."
—John 8:9–11

Jesus spoke with such conviction. In such a brief span of time the woman had gone from someone condemned to someone set free. She no longer stood in fear. There was no more name calling, no eyes filled with hate, and no disgrace. Instead the eyes of Jesus embraced her with forgiveness and love—a love that promised a new beginning.

In our next story a woman finds the courage to face her painful past.

Need to Forgive
Dr. Mary M. Simms

Marley was a 42-year-old woman who came to me with symptoms of depression and anxiety related to her marital struggles. She had been to several therapists already, and when she found me, she seemed at the end of her rope.

"I am tired," she said with a sigh.

"What does that mean?" I asked. "Are you tired of your circumstances, or are you tired of your life?"

"Both," she exclaimed, "I just wish I would go to sleep and never wake up."

"Well," I replied, "I know you feel this way at the moment, but tomorrow you might wake up feeling differently. There is a Bible verse that says, *'You [God] turned my wailing into dancing; you removed my sackcloth and clothed me with joy'*" (Psalm 30:11).

"Well, right now I am weary."

Studying my evaluation of her, I had reason to suspect that Marley could hurt herself because she had attempted suicide once several years before. She took a bottle of pain relievers and went into a deep sleep. Her husband came home and called 911. She was in the hospital for three weeks. After intensive group and individual therapy, she had been on the mend.

Marley described her suicide attempt. "It was a time in my life when I was in a very dark place. I felt so alone, so isolated, and I thought no one loved me. I know I really didn't like myself either. I just wanted to end it all."

After several therapy sessions, I learned her stepfather had sexually abused her. The abuse began at the tender age of 7 and ended when Marley turned 13. The abuse happened when her mom worked night shifts and the stepdad was home. It became obvious to me that her marital problems were related to the sexual abuse she'd endured as a child. That abuse not only affected her marriage negatively but many other areas of her life.

Shy and quiet, she carried a lot of shame related to the sexual abuse. Marley internalized her negative feelings. Helping her to express herself would be difficult.

In her childhood, when things got bad, she protected herself by pretending that she lived somewhere else and imagined a life apart from what she was currently experiencing.

As we continued working together, we discovered that she still employed the same coping mechanisms that she did when she was a child. When she became afraid, she buried her real feelings deep within her. Then she coped by internalizing her feelings and pretending that those feelings did not exist. Once she shut down, she could not respond to the people in her life who were safe and close to her, those who wanted to help her.

During our time together Marley did not seem to develop any hope at all. She saw things as dark much of the time. The good news was that she did have a personal relationship with Jesus, and she often prayed to Him when she felt trapped in a dark and enclosed place.

I asked her, "When you feel closed in, does Jesus bring any light to you?"

"Yes. As a little girl I often hid in the closet when my stepdad came into my room. I prayed to God to help me, and many times he fell asleep in my bed because he had been drinking. I escaped his wrath by sleeping under the bed during those times. Also, when I turned 13, my mom got a job in another state, and she decided to break up with him. I felt relief over her decision. I see now that God's hand was on my life even when I was a little girl and felt trapped and powerless."

"Were you ever able to tell your mom about the abuse?"

"No. I thought I needed to protect Mom's feelings. She worked awfully hard for me. Besides, when my stepdad left, I thought we could go on with our lives."

Unfortunately, Marley could not go on with her life in a healthy way without seeing how the abuse affected her as an adult. As we worked together, she began to see that not only had she been violated sexually, which was affecting her marital relationship, but also her God-given voice was taken from her at an early age because of the violation. As she found the courage to connect her painful feelings without fear, she began to find her voice again.

"I am getting better at handling my emotions," Marley said. "Before, if I felt anger, I would just bury it and think I wanted to die. I wanted to run away or just go away forever. Now I'm not afraid to allow a negative emotion to surface. My husband is going to be relieved. I have been placing a lot of the anger on him that I now know was meant for my stepdad. I am not afraid to work through my anger at my stepdad anymore."

As Marley began to gradually deal with her anger toward the man who had violated her, she also got in touch with her own anger and self-hatred. She realized that she had been beating herself up over what had been done to her.

She had difficulty forgiving herself, but when Marley imagined a violation happening to her seven-year-old daughter, she realized she had a lot of empathy. As we worked on helping her develop empathy toward herself, she began to let go of the anger and started developing more self-acceptance and self-empowerment.

Marley discovered that journaling helped her to look at a lot of those ugly emotions that were buried inside, which caused her to act out in self-destructive ways. She finally developed the courage to write a letter to her stepdad to get out her feelings. The letter pulled up all the negative emotions, anger, and rage that were buried deep inside.

After she wrote the letter, Marley shared, "It's a letter that was written to help me release what happened. It is so full of venom and poison that I would become just like him if I mailed it. I now know I have a long way to go toward forgiving him and forgiving myself, but God is giving me the grace to work toward forgiveness. I know I need to take this step if I want to be free and enjoy healthy relationships."

☀ ☀ ☀

Words from Jeenie

Never will I forget a client who was sexually abused as a tiny child until puberty. She, too, wanted to end the pain in her life and was suicidal.

One day I asked, "Do you believe you were somehow responsible for the sexual abuse?" I sensed her answer.

Hanging her head in silence, she finally whispered, "Yes."

I responded, "In what way?"

Again, she sat without speaking. With shame in her eyes, she barely lifted her head and replied, "Well, I guess I was sexy."

Shocked, I exclaimed, "Sexy! You were five years old. You were not sexy!"

I asked her to bring in several photos of herself as a little girl for the next session. As we looked at the precious, innocent face of a five- to ten-year-old child, she was able to understand and accept she had been violated and was totally innocent. Thus, began her journey toward wholeness.

Sexual, physical, and emotional abuse must be dealt with in therapy. Those who do not deal with it often believe they cannot go on living with the underlying intense pain. Sadly, some choose not to live.

Reflections

1. Do you still feel some resentment surrounding the death of a loved one? Make a list of those resentments and then, one-by-one, ask God to help you to forgive.

2. Perhaps you attempted suicide and now struggle with the consequences. Ask God to help you forgive yourself.

Prayer

Lord, when others accused me, You forgave me. When doubt clouded my mind, You reminded me of why Christ died. When my heart ached with self-condemnation, You gave me Your love and grace. Help me to treat others with the same compassion and forgiveness. In Jesus's name I pray, amen.

CHAPTER 11

THE COURAGE
TO GO ON

Be on guard. Stand firm in the faith. Be courageous. Be strong.
—1 Corinthians 16:13 (NLT)

Problems and suffering enter every life sooner or later. These come in many forms, silently at times and like a sonic boom at others. What's important is what we do about our circumstances. Are we snowed under and unable to get up, or do we dig our way out and go on with our lives? The truth is we need strength beyond our own to go on. This can only come from God. Faith in God produces hope, and hope builds a bridge that leads to courage.

Cynthia McClure learned these truths in her remarkable life. There had been a time when she struggled secretly with bingeing and purging. Cynthia had gone to 15 different doctors, and none were able to help her. "I can't go on," she reasoned. At this point she made a plan to kill herself.

But before she was able to carry out her plan, a friend called and said, "Cynthia, a lady came to our church and talked about eating disorders. She said there is a hospital in Texas that can probably help you. Here's the number for that facility."

The first two weeks after Cynthia admitted herself, she was kept on a heart monitor. Due to her eating disorder, her electrolytes were dangerously low. Cynthia remained in the hospital for three months in intense therapy. Gradually, with the help of her therapist, the reasons behind her eating problem surfaced.

After being discharged, Cynthia announced her plans. "I am going to write a book." She then left behind her career as a television news reporter and began a ministry called Helping the Hungry Heart. For 18 years, she reached out to others in the throes of eating disorders. As an inspirational speaker, she traveled and spoke at churches nationwide.

Then cancer raised its ugly head. Cynthia's doctor said, "The cancer is in your lungs and bones." He gave her only a few months to live.

But Cynthia didn't lie down and die as they had predicted. In between chemotherapy and other treatments, she continued to speak, raising money for cancer research.

Five years passed, and Cynthia continued to fight the cancer that raged in her body. Then she developed pneumonia and was hospitalized. Soon, with her family at her side, she slipped into a coma.

Those who knew and loved Cynthia witnessed her courage, love, and devotion toward others. Cynthia's choice to live saved more than her own life. Many lives were spared from eating disorders. She left behind a legacy of courage and faith.

COURAGE ON STRAIGHT STREET

Ananias also left a legacy of courage, and we find his story in Acts 9. But before we can deeply appreciate Ananias, we need to place ourselves on the road to Damascus with a man named Saul of Tarsus.

Each step forward on the road to Damascus fueled the determination in Saul's murderous heart to find and destroy those who followed Jesus Christ. He carried with him letters from the high priest to present to the synagogues in Damascus—letters that gave Saul the authority he needed to seek out and take captive converts to what was considered a dangerous new belief. He planned to take women and men back to Jerusalem to imprison them. He was not looking for a miracle that would convert his own heart.

As he neared Damascus on his journey, suddenly a light from heaven flashed around him. He fell to the ground and heard a voice say to him, "Saul, Saul, why do you persecute me?"

"Who are you, Lord?" Saul asked.

"I am Jesus, whom you are persecuting," he replied. "Now get up and go into the city, and you will be told what you must do."

The men traveling with Saul stood there speechless; they heard the sound but did not see anyone. Saul got up from the ground, but when he opened his eyes he could see nothing. So they led him by the hand into Damascus. For three days he was blind, and did not eat or drink anything

—Acts 9:3–9

While these incredible events were taking place, a disciple named Ananias went about his normal routines. Unaware and unsuspecting, he didn't realize that God would soon call on him to become a part of an extraordinary plan.

The Lord called to him in a vision, "Ananias."

"Yes, Lord," he answered.

The Lord told him, "Go to the house of Judas on Straight Street and ask for a man from Tarsus named Saul, for he is praying. In a vision he has seen a man named Ananias come and place his hands on him to restore his sight."

"Lord," Ananias answered, "I have heard many reports about this man and all the harm he has done to your saints in Jerusalem. And he has come here with authority from the chief priests to arrest all who call on your name."

But the Lord said to Ananias, "Go! This man is my chosen instrument to carry my name before the Gentiles and their kings and before the people of Israel. I will show him how much he must suffer for my name."

Then Ananias went to the house and entered it. Placing his hands on Saul, he said, "Brother Saul, the Lord—Jesus, who appeared to you on the road as you were coming here—has sent me so that you may see again and be filled with the Holy Spirit." Immediately, something like scales fell from Saul's eyes, and he could see again. He got up and was baptized, and after taking some food, he regained his strength

—Acts 9:10–19

Ananias acted in a courageous way and even referred to Saul as his brother. From a life filled with hate and a determination to destroy followers of Christ, Saul was transformed into Paul, an apostle of Christ.

There's no doubt it takes courage to move forward in life after an attempted suicide or the loss of a loved one. Life takes on a more profound meaning—with a new responsibility to help others value their lives. God brings us to the brink of sorrow and back. He calls on us to embrace each day with obedience and love. To save lives takes strength beyond our own. His courage fills us with hope and a love for life that is beyond description. God has written on our hearts, "Go and live life to the fullest. Love my people."

In the following story Karen finds the courage to go on when memories resurfaced during the holidays.

Let Me Forget

Karen Kosman

Thanksgiving was quickly approaching, bringing with it the memory of Robbie's death now forever intertwined with this holiday. It had been six years, but I didn't want to think about it. *Haven't I grieved enough? I don't want to feel this pain again,* my mind screamed.

At work, while my boss was on medical leave, I'd stepped into the role of supervisor over the phlebotomy technicians. This new assignment, along with my responsibilities to train new employees, kept me very busy. On this particular day, with my emotions surfacing, I felt vulnerable. I loved my job, but felt anxious to go home.

I finished the timecards and turned them in. Looking up at the clock, I felt relieved. Finally I could leave.

Exhaustion overtook me by the time I pulled into our driveway. As I stepped out of my car, a wonderful smell enticed me from our kitchen window. *God bless, John,* I thought. He's *cooked dinner, but how do I tell him I'm too tired to eat?*

John took one look at me and asked, "Karen, are you all right?"

"Yes," I replied, "I'm just tired."

After dinner we watched a little TV and then I retired, hoping that sleep was what I needed. John left for work the next morning before I got up. Later he told me, "When I left that morning, you were sleeping peacefully."

I don't remember anything that happened after I woke up. My only record comes from what others told me later. Apparently, I called work and asked a secretary, "What day is it?"

Concerned for my well-being, she called my daughter, Linda. Linda then called me, and I asked her the same question. Linda realized I was disoriented, and she called the paramedics, who took me to the nearest hospital.

Awareness of my surroundings didn't come until that evening. Suddenly I realized I had an IV in my arm. Then I looked up into my husband's concerned eyes. "John, why am I here?"

"Karen, they called me at work and said you'd been rushed to the hospital. You couldn't remember anything. When they asked you your name, you told them, but you didn't know where you were."

Just then a doctor walked into the cubicle. "Welcome back, Karen. I'm Dr. Jennings. You were brought in with a lapse of memory. We're going to keep you here a while and run some tests to make sure you didn't have a stroke."

I nodded my head, totally confused about the whole situation. A short time later, my daughter joined us in the ER.

"Mom, you sounded so confused this morning. You didn't remember the conversation that we had last night about Robbie. Nor did you realize you'd called your work this morning."

"I can't explain what happened, Linda, but don't worry, I'm in good hands. I know you are expecting my second grandbaby anytime now."

Later that night I was moved to a hospital room where I finally got some sleep. The next morning I awoke to the phone ringing next to my bed. When I answered it, I heard my daughter's excited voice. "Mom, you have a new granddaughter, Staci Louise."

"Oh, Linda, that's wonderful. Are you and the baby doing OK?"

"Yes, it was an easy delivery. I only wish you'd been here to see her born like you were when I gave birth to Breanna. Mom, get better soon so you can meet your new granddaughter."

"I plan on it, Linda."

Three days later my doctor released me, and I went home. The doorbell rang, and when I walked to the door, I saw Linda standing there with a big grin—holding Staci.

"Oh, let me have that baby girl," I said, laughing. I took Staci in my arms, holding her tightly as I sat down on the couch. Linda had her dressed in a yellow bunting with little rabbit ears.

I felt so blessed to have beautiful grandchildren. Somehow it made it easier to deal with the memories of Robbie.

A week later I waited while a neurologist glanced at my medical reports. He leaned forward and said, "Karen, what you experienced is called transient global amnesia. We don't know what causes it, but it is a temporary memory loss that isn't attributed to a more serious condition, such as epilepsy, transient ischemic attack, stroke, or head injury."

"Will it happen again?" I asked, both relieved and concerned at the same time.

"Don't worry. The condition is rare, and among the few who do have one episode, a second occurrence is uncommon."

He seemed to think there was no connection between the emotions I'd felt about Robbie and the amnesia, but I wondered....

Later, that night, I prayed, "Lord, I know You understand grief and loss. I realize now that there are going to be moments when those sad memories return. But thank You for teaching me how precious memories are. I'm thankful for the life we shared with Robbie. Give me courage to go forward with the plans You have for my life."

When Thanksgiving arrived, we all shared memories of Robbie. Laughter filled the room, and God's grace filled me with courage.

Strangely enough, after my brief bout with amnesia, I knew I needed to reach out and comfort others who had lost loved ones from suicide. In faith, I waited for God to give me His guidance, so I'd be ready to step forward.

☀ ☀ ☀

Words from Jeenie

Both Cynthia and Karen found the courage to go on. We can all expect trauma in our lives. Yet it is vital to strive toward wholeness—spiritual and emotional health.

I'd like to share the following story about that first Thanksgiving after my painful divorce. My daughter and I didn't look forward to spending that day alone.

"I'm going to fix a big dinner and invite students from Biola University," I told my daughter. The word spread, and about a dozen students came.

As I was putting on the finishing touches to the meal, one young man quietly said, "When I was leaving the dorm, there was a guy just sitting there."

"Well, go get him," I said, and he did.

Even though we were all strangers, we had a wonderful day. It was filled with laughter and lots of food. We played games and talked about our lives.

I learned these students were missionary kids, across the globe from home and would have been alone on their first Thanksgiving at college. Years later, one of the young men told me, "That was the best Thanksgiving I ever had."

When we reach out to others, even in our pain, it aids in our healing.

In the next story a mother shares how a memory of her daughter helped her set new goals for her own life.

"Go for It, Mom"
Mary Bradbury

Five months ago, my eldest daughter, Paulette, took her own life. She had attempted this several times in the last 12 years, but this time she accomplished her goal.

It began when she was diagnosed with a mental illness (schizoid affective disorder). She was hospitalized many times during those years. Medications were adjusted and new ones introduced. One negative side effect of these psychotropic drugs was weight gain. During treatment she gained more than 125 pounds, which contributed to her depression.

There were times in her life when the medications seemed to work, and she'd feel better. I treasure the memories of those moments. We went shopping together and stopped at our favorite coffee shop. I know she felt my love as we sat and talked. I kissed the top of her head and said, "Paulette, I love you."

I also find peace in knowing that in fifth grade Paulette accepted Christ as her Savior. During her long illness, her faith brought her through many trying times.

Shortly after my daughter's death, thoughts of her constantly filled my mind. Several times I asked myself, "Do you believe that Christ died for you?" *Yes.* "Do you believe in eternal life?" *Yes.* "Do you believe Paulette is safe in the arms of our Lord?" *Of course I do.* These conversations with myself gave me solace. Many times, I could almost hear her say, "Mom, I'm OK. Enjoy your life."

Several things have comforted me during these past five months. Seeing how other people who have lost children are getting on with their lives has helped. As one of my friends, whose son died from suicide, said, "You get through it, but you never get over it." Another friend wrote, "No more dark days for Paulette, only happy days with Jesus."

Every few days after she died, God seemed to give me insight into her death.

I am comforted as I look at pictures of Paulette—pictures of happy times. My favorite is one taken a year ago, when she visited us in Oregon. Barefooted and holding a soda, she had a beautiful, serene look on her face as she sat among other family members. As I look at this picture, I kiss it and whisper, *I love you, Paulette.*

Not everyone grieves the same way. I have never been embarrassed in front of others if the tears fall. They are tears of love for my sweet daughter.

Those same memories give me courage to move on with my life. I have set some new goals in my life. Ten years ago I wrote a book. Paulette was the only one who read it in its entirety. I have started a writers group where I live and now am working on the rewrite of that book. This has kept me focused, and I can almost hear Paulette saying, "Go for it, Mom."

※ ※ ※

Words from Jeenie

One Sunday after coming home from church, I listened to my voice mail.

"Jeenie," sobbed Mary, "Paulette took her own life."

Mary and I had been close friends for 25 years. At Paulette's memorial service, Mary requested that I read a special rendition of Psalm 23:

The Lord is my Shepherd—that's relationship.
I shall not want—that's supply.
He maketh me to lie down in green pastures—that's rest.
He leadeth me beside the still waters—that's refreshment.
He restoreth my soul—that's healing.
He leadeth me in the paths of righteousness—that's guidance.

For His name's sake—that's purpose.

Yea, though I walk through the valley of the shadow of death—that's testing.

I will fear no evil—that's protection.

For Thou art with me—that's faithfulness.

Thy rod and Thy staff they comfort me—that's discipline.

Thou preparest a table before me in the presence of mine enemies—that's hope.

Thou anointest my head with oil—that's consecration.

My cup runneth over—that's abundance.

Surely goodness and mercy shall follow me all the days of my life—that's blessing.

And I will dwell in the house of the Lord—that's security.

Forever—that's eternity!

In the following story L. B. also finds the courage to go on after her husband takes his own life in Germany.

A Different Kind of Family

L. B. Greer

"Staff Sergeant Greer never reported for duty this morning," said Garson's commanding officer on the telephone. "Do you know where he is?"

"No, I have no idea," I replied.

"Are you having any problems?"

"No, of course not. Last night, we just cuddled on the couch watching TV."

After hanging up, I thought back to the sudden and inexplicable foreboding that awoke me that morning bringing a sense of dread. Garson had already left for work.

Instinctively, I searched for the bullets for his pistol. They were missing. I knelt and tearfully prayed, "Lord, please let my husband be found. Let him be safe." To keep my mind off the sinking feeling in the pit of my stomach, I unpacked the last box from our recent transatlantic move to Germany.

That night the chaplain and two officers delivered the most painful news of my life. Garson's body was found in the woods, midway between our German home and the post, with a self-inflicted gunshot wound to the head. He'd died instantly.

"I'll let the girls sleep for one more night believing they still have a daddy. I will tell Anna and Dina in the morning," I said before closing the door softly behind kind men. Suddenly I was thrown onto the edge of an incomparably strong vortex of depression. I thought, *All my dreams have ended. All my love has been sucked out of me. My life is over... over... over.*

My girls and I immediately returned to the US. Eleven days after our arrival in Virginia, Garson's body arrived. We were staying with my sister, her husband, and their three sons. The few belongings we brought with us, packed in such haste after Garson's memorial service in Germany, only served to remind me of the holes in my life. I suffered from a severely broken heart and held all of my being together with spider-web fragility.

Then my daughter Anna smashed her hand in the swing set. My nephew rushed us to the military clinic. As I spoke with Anna's doctor, the fragile web wrapped around my emotions broke and the tears wouldn't stop. So he ended up treating both Anna and me.

The doctor looked at me and said, "I'm admitting you to the hospital."

The psych ward added to my loneliness. The first weekend in the hospital I spent in silence, unable to voice the horror of my widowhood, let alone my family's lack of understanding and their denial of my grief.

I was broken for all to see, but my family couldn't see, wouldn't see. They had become monsters with stone hearts and thought they had the answers. "You have all that insurance money now. Just get on with your life! Make some decisions!"

Two weeks later, with nowhere else to go, I returned to my sister's home in a taxicab. A short time later a captain at a nearby army installation was assigned as my casualty assistance officer. He said, "I've made plans for you to fly to North Carolina and stay with your brother, Brad, and his wife."

I traveled alone, after shoving $300 into my sister's hand and leaving my little girls in the temporary care of her family. Brad's trailer home, located 30 miles outside of Fort Bragg, would allow me to search for housing in Fayetteville.

On my arrival, Brad offered, "L. B., you can use my old car."

On my second trip into Fayetteville, the brakes failed as I approached an intersection. I coasted through a red light holding my breath. The car was summarily parked, and my realtor drove me to Brad's home after a tiring, unsuccessful day of house hunting. As we passed the place where the car had been deserted, I saw that strong arms had deposited it on the grassy curb. It seems the car was blocking traffic, and some GIs decided to literally take matters into their own hands. "I wondered, *Would a pair of arms ever hold me again?*

Two weeks of unsuccessful house searching forced me into a sparsely furnished rental townhouse in Fayetteville. My sister refused to drive to North Carolina with my children. I had to arrange a rendezvous midway, so I rented a used car for the trip.

Our luncheon meeting was icy. I refused to look into my sister's eyes. I knew she resented traveling even this far to help me. I took solace in knowing that two little girls were happy to see me. For the first time since my husband's suicide, I smiled with my arms ready to hug my daughters. With renewed hope, I understood that I wanted to live—to be a stronghold for Anna and Dina.

"Girls, I want you to know that I will never leave you. God hasn't left us alone either." I knew healing would take time, but I felt determined with God's help, and all of my being, to assure them we were still a family.

☀ ☀ ☀

Words from Jeenie

Over and over I've seen tears flow down the sad face of a client who was rejected by a family member in a time of great need. Sometimes we cannot count on those closest to us. L.B. experienced a rude and cruel awakening due to her sister's lack of empathy. The warmth and comfort she desperately needed were never realized. Only people who have not suffered greatly can be so calloused and unconcerned.

I believe God looks on such situations with a heart of love and provides through unexpected means. The captain arranged for L.B.'s flight to North Carolina to be with her brother. Brad offered shelter and his car to assist in her search for housing. God even brought along some strong GIs to move her inoperable car out of traffic.

Sometimes our family may desert us, but Scripture states God promises to never abandon us, *"Even if my father and mother abandon me, the Lord will hold me close"* (Psalm 27:10 NLT).

We can count on God's faithfulness.

HOLD ON!
Charles R. Brown

What an amazing thing, God.
It blows my mind
to think that You grabbed me,
You took hold of me
and have told me You will not let go.
Truly, all other things profitable
are not what they appear to be
when placed beside the knowledge of you.
Knowing You is the best of the best.

All else is trash.
I have found a treasure in You.
O, dear Father, I want to know You more.
Blessed Jesus, I want to see Your face.
Holy Spirit, I want to be filled to overflowing.
Take hold, again, Lord,
as I push ahead and take hold of You.
You know my weakness,
my tendency toward letting go.
Even then You hold me still.
You will not let me go.
No rapids can drown my
relationship with You.
You are my rescuer, my guide, my salvation.
I *will* hold on!

———

I press on to take hold of that for which Christ Jesus took hold of me.
—Philippians 3:12

In the following story, Wanda tells of her friend Carol's struggle with the death of her sister, Angie, who even left a note blaming her. However, through God's grace, Carol gained new courage.

Choices
Wanda J. Burnside

All my life I had planned to go to college. I cared about my academic achievement and the dean's list, but I wanted to have a good time in college too. During freshman orientation, I met some nice people. It felt great being with them in class and, at lunchtime, studying together and just hanging around campus.

In one of my classes, a girl kept staring at me. I couldn't help but notice how thin and fragile she looked. I tried to make eye contact with her, but she always turned away. After a while, I decided to ignore her so I sat on the other side of the room.

One day after class, she stepped in front of me. Clutching her stack of books close to her chest, she said, "Hi! I'm Carol."

"Hi! I'm Wanda," I replied.

She smiled, then looked away.

"Hey, Wanda!" I heard someone call out, "Are you going to the student union with us for lunch?"

I turned to see a group of my friends from class motioning to me. "Yeah, I'm coming," I answered.

"Go on," said Carol. "Don't let me stop you."

"No. Please come with us. Let's talk," I said.

"Well, I don't know . . ." she hesitated and then continued, "I usually . . ."

"Wanda, come on and bring your friend," said Charles.

So we ran to catch up with the others. My friends accepted Carol, and from that day on, she went everywhere with us. She transformed from someone painfully shy to someone outgoing. Everybody saw the difference in her. Even the professors made comments about her budding personality.

By the end of our freshman year, Carol made friends on her own and joined several campus clubs.

One day, a group of us decided to walk to a new restaurant across the street from the campus. As we reached the parking lot, up drove a shiny red convertible. "Carol!" shouted a pretty girl with flowing hair. She got out of the car. "Carol!"

Carol stood frozen with a look of fear and sheer desperation on her face. Her hands began to shake. Her eyes filled with tears, and for several moments she remained silent.

The other girl wore colorful, tight-fitting clothes that clung to her curves. Plus she had a beautiful, flawless complexion.

"Carol! Today's my birthday! Remember? My friends are coming over tonight, and you promised to decorate for my party! Why are you here? I told Mama you'd ruin everything for me. You, your good grades, and your school!" she yelled.

"This is my sister, Angie," Carol softly said with tears rolling down her face. "Excuse me, everyone." Then they got into the car and drove away.

"Carol never mentioned her sister," Charles commented. "They're so opposite."

"Hey, what was that all about?" asked Tyrone.

"Angie is a fox, and Carol's so skinny!" Terry laughed.

"Hey, guys. Stop! Carol is our friend," said Barbara.

"Next week, after this Angie's party blows over, I'll give Carol a call," said Ebony.

Two weeks passed, and Carol had not returned to school. Several of us tried to phone her, but no one could reach her. We all wondered what happened.

One evening while doing my homework at home, my mother called me to the phone.

I listened to a distraught voice. "I'm Carol's mom. My daughter...she died. Life isn't the same without my beautiful daughter," she cried.

"Carol died?" I asked.

Another voice came on the phone. "Hello, Wanda."

"Carol. Carol, is it you? What is going on?"

"My sister, Angie...she killed herself. She drove into our garage, rolled up the windows, and left the engine running. She also left a long letter—one that blamed me. Angie said I had everything—friends, good grades, and a boyfriend."

I couldn't believe it. *Angie, dead?*

Shortly after our phone conversation, Carol dropped out of school. We later learned she was hospitalized for depression. None of us knew what to do. Carol's absence created a void in all our lives.

A year later, Carol called me. "Hi, Wanda, this is Carol."

"Carol," I hesitated, "how are you?"

"I'm fine. I'm living in California and attending college. I'm also engaged."

"Carol, you sound happy. I'm so glad for you." I continued, "We've all missed you."

"Yeah, Wanda, I miss all of you, too. You know, I turned to God. My sister's jealousy and hatred caused me a lot of pain. Yet, I'll always miss her. God helped me to accept the unacceptable. Angie chose to die. I choose to live."

Carol later received a doctorate in psychology, got married, had children, and opened a clinic to help troubled teens.

☼ ☼ ☼

Words from Jeenie

How amazing that Carol could overcome the horrific blame her sister, Angie, laid on her. Rarely does that happen. Only God's intervention can explain it.

Occasionally, a suicide note such as Angie's is left. Sometimes, it is a last attempt for vengeance. It appears Angie had probably been jealous of her sister for years—jealous of her good grades and desire to earn a college education. Somehow, in Angie's twisted thinking, she did not measure up to her sister so she seethed with anger. It likely was self-loathing that she projected onto unsuspecting, undeserving Carol.

Undoubtedly, Carol is now a therapist whose life, understanding, and influence will save teens from the road Angie chose to take. My prayer is that God would increase her number in our profession.

REFLECTIONS

1. Write down the fears you have about your future.

2. Close your eyes and picture Jesus removing the burdens of doubt and fear from your heart. In place of despair, He offers courage. You don't have to face tomorrow alone.

Prayer

*Thank You, Lord, for surrounding me with Your presence.
You have provided me with courage and the ability to face tomorrow.
In Jesus's name I pray, amen.*

CHAPTER 12

FREE TO LIVE AGAIN

"Then you will know the truth, and the truth will set you free."
—John 8:32

E ach dawn gives birth to a new day. When the sun rises, the dark shadows of night are chased away. Rays of sunlight bring warmth and comfort, calling out to those they touch, "You are set free to live one more day. Use your time wisely."

Elaina's family experienced renewal. They were set free once again to love one another and embrace the world with laughter and joy. But at one point, after Elaina's brother's suicide, a dark cloud seemed to hang over her heart. Michael's final words rang again in her mind, haunting her. "I am such a failure."

The storm clouds of despair had followed Michael for so long. After he was released from the hospital, everyone hoped he'd remain on his medication and find happiness again. But in one despairing moment, he ended it all. Elaina's mind screamed, *How could Michael leave behind his loved ones—especially his beautiful little girl?*

Elaina never dreamt that in two years she and her husband would take custody of their seven-year-old niece. But when it became obvious that Rose's mom was incapable of caring for her, Elaina and her husband fought hard to gain custody so they could give her a loving home.

Soon after Rose came to live with them, they took her to the local bike shop, and she picked out a new powder-blue bike. They ended up buying three bikes that day. When Elaina got on her new bike, she didn't get far. She fell off, scraping her knee, and thought, *That puts an end to my bike riding.*

But Rose, with a smile and trusting eyes said, "Get up, Aunt Elaina. Get back on your bike."

Before long they were riding bike trails together. Elaina heard another Voice saying to her, *Live life to the fullest.*

When asked by a friend what she would say to Michael if she could, Elaina responded, "Michael, do not regret the fact that you had Rose. She is beautiful, a blessing to everyone who knows and loves her. She has such a zest for life. At 12 she shows a deep compassion toward others and wisdom far beyond her age. Someday Rose wants to be a veterinarian. She gets good grades in school, so I believe she'll accomplish her goal. Trusting God and loving Rose have set me free to live again. I only wish, Michael, that you could be here with us. There are times when my tears fall for you, but God wipes them away and gives me determination to live by faith."

God is lovingly waiting for anyone who has lived in despair to embrace a new day.

Words from Jeenie

Many of us can empathize with Elaina. Once we fall, we do not want to get up. Climbing back on the bike is hard. First learning to ride a bike is not easy. We wobble and tumble many times. Our feet keep slipping off the pedals, so we look down instead of seeing what's ahead. Then, there are the handlebars. They wiggle from side to side as we attempt to hold them steady. The more we practice, the better we become. Before long, we master the technique of riding a bicycle.

Getting up from gut-wrenching emotional pain seems impossible. However, it's the only way we will eventually find a sense of peace. What we do will determine the outcome. The more we persevere and move toward wholeness, the sooner some relief will emerge.

Many times in our lives, we shoot up a prayer of hope: "Lord, somehow You and I are going to get through this together." And, we do.

THE OTHER SIDE
C.A.N.

Miles of darkness everywhere I turned—
Then I saw light on the other side.
I slowly approached, curious indeed.
But looking forward to the other side
I saw a shadow, but I didn't shudder.
For I knew it was You, Lord, on the other side.
No words can explain the way I felt
When I finally met You on the other side.

Although Shelly lost her mother at the tender age of seven, she turned that tragedy into a vocation of helping children with special needs.

In a Moment
Shelly Moran

"Your mother went to heaven last night," my daddy said, and with that he started to cry. And I giggled, just a little for a moment, because I thought *he* might be giggling. I'd never seen him cry—couldn't fathom or recognize it. I imagine, to a seven-year-old, the possibility had never occurred.

We sat at the table that morning, with my sister, Jessica (eight), and brother, Patrick (six), and we cried. Actually, Patrick didn't cry, he just looked bewildered.

"Why aren't you crying?" Jessica screamed at him.

Unlike Patrick, I understood. In a moment, Mama had been torn from my life permanently.

"She tripped," Daddy said, by way of explanation. "She tripped over the rug and hurt her brain." I remembered later telling my friends at school the fall had knocked her brain to the other side of her head. I sat against the wall at recess, watching these kids talk and looking over their shoulders at me. I had become a celebrity of sorts: a tragic, desolate figure in their small underdeveloped worlds where tragedy was still rare.

I withdrew. She died in March, five days after her 29th birthday, and that summer we moved, changing houses and schools. In my new third-grade class I had no friends, and I no longer played. Daddy never spoke of her and disengaged as well. I made my first bad grade and wrote in pencil on my desk, "I made an F." Although my teacher confronted me, I denied the transgression, and she never pursued it. I must have thought I fooled her.

One morning of the summer we moved Daddy pulled to the side of the road on the way to my grandmother's house. "Your mother didn't fall. She shot herself." He went on to say how he didn't think we could handle the truth that day, but he wanted us to know now. From that moment to this, I've often reflected with awe upon all he must have gone through.

I prayed hard, believing for about a year that if I prayed *enough*, God might bring my mother back. I knew He could do anything. I also had two recurring dreams. In one, she had on my favorite dress: a belted, full-skirted sleeveless one, covered in large red roses, so typically 1960s. She'd taken Jessica and me to the sidewalk so we could walk to school. But not far along my way, some wolves snatched me into a hole in the embankment. They lay me down and began to scrape the skin off my back. Out of the corner of my eye, I saw Jessica disappearing up the hill to school and Mama climbing the steps to the house. "Mama!" I screamed over and over, but the wolves, with their oddly human voices, said, "She doesn't hear you, and she'll never come for you."

In the other dream Mama, sporting her silky, dark brown pageboy, was riding in a jalopy, like the car in *Chitty Chitty Bang Bang*. Four handsome boys, who looked like the Beatles, surrounded her. They came to meet me for lime sours, just like we used to order after ballet class. Mama sat on the stool beside me, laughing and talking. I kept repeating things like, "That's great, Mama, but when are you coming home?" But she acted like she couldn't hear me. I grew insistent, but she continued to laugh and talk and toss her pretty, shiny hair.

Then the boys gathered around her and announced, "It's time to go." She told me goodbye, smiled, and sailed away in her movie-star car with her movie-star friends. And I cried, "Mama, come back!" but she never turned around—not even once.

I lied about her death until I was 20. I said she was sick and that I remembered visiting her in the hospital. There was so much shame surrounding the suicide, and as adults, we found out cousins on both sides had been told, "Never mention Aunt Marlene." The fact that some believed her act had condemned her to hell only added to our agony.

When someone you love dies, it turns your life upside down in a way from which you think you'll never recover. It's only through time that you realize this broken life *is* your life, the life God has given you. But He will stretch and love you through it all. I came to Christ at age 12, while catching a ride on a church bus, and have since learned God is in charge of the world, of me, and of the soul of my Christian, hurting, desperate, loving, impulsive mother. I will never totally understand what happened or why, and I am not meant to, but I am meant to remember God loves her and me, as much as He loves His Son. My job is to trust Him, knowing God has a purpose for us all.

In the course of my life, without my knowing it, I developed a love for hurting people. This empathy expresses itself not only through teaching special education, but also when I'm open, through daily opportunities of small compassions. As a Christian, I realize my broken heart was somehow strengthened through Christ's mercy, and now I feel compelled to share His love through my own hands, my feet, and my words.

☀ ☀ ☀

Words from Jeenie

As I deal with many men in therapy, it is not unusual for them to have difficulty relating emotionally. Moms are more often the ones who bind the physical and emotional wounds of children.

As with Shelly, her father knew no other way but to blurt out the truth to his children. He did not know exactly what to say or do to comfort them.

Children must be given the truth, but it must be age-appropriate. Seven is far too young to be told many things. The father should have only dealt with the fact that Shelly's mommy had died. He could have spoken about God taking her to heaven and that someday they would all be together again. (Note: I tend to agree with other professionals that if the child is told about the suicide by others, then the parent does need to deal with it at that time. Otherwise it is best left unsaid until the child is older.)

Crying with children gives them permission to cry. Also, holding a child in one's arms brings comfort to that child. Talking often about the deceased parent and teaching the children to remember the good times helps them to process their pain.

Later in Shelly's life, she would have wanted more information and undoubtedly have asked for it. At that time, she would have been more ready to receive the truth. Then, they could discuss the fact that her mother undoubtedly had a moment of insanity and made a quick and irreversible decision—emphasizing that suicide is never the answer.

Because of the devastating effect the death of Shelly's mother had on her, she isolated herself, and the loneliness smothered her like a heavy blanket until a small community church came to the rescue and covered her with love. Only then did Shelly and her siblings find wholeness in Christ.

Linda Davis tells how her daughter made the choice to overcome emotional and physical trauma and today leads a normal, healthy life.

When I See Her Scars
Linda B. Davis

My daughter's wrists are scarred. Her scars speak of the pain of shame, rejection, and death.

Linda Lee was overweight from age 8 to age 12. During that time, her classmates inflicted lifelong wounds. Their "Miss Piggy" taunts said, *You are not as good as the rest of us.* Although the taunts were short-lived, Linda Lee simply absorbed the abuse and buried the hurt.

Doctors point to one violent event in 1986, however, as the most devastating event in Linda Lee's life. During a friend's sleepover, a 25-year-old man who was acquainted with her friend's family raped her. He caught Linda Lee, 15 at the time, alone, and in a matter of minutes shattered her young life.

Filled with shame, Linda Lee hid her secret—even from herself. Over the next three and one-half years, however, her secret festered and came close to claiming her life.

In 1989 Linda Lee was hospitalized with an eating disorder that grew from the agonizing pain inside her. When they admitted her, hospital staff overlooked a compact in her purse. Within two weeks, she broke the mirror and used it to slash her wrists. Thankfully, a staff member found her before she accomplished her goal.

During the showing of a date rape film as part of a hospital group therapy session, Linda Lee's memory resurfaced.

"I suddenly remembered what that man did to me…the fear, the pain, the shame," she told me the next day. "I remembered being surprised that I couldn't move. I thought a woman could get away if she wanted to, but that's not true. He was way too big and too strong. I felt like a piece of dirt, Mom."

By the grace of God, Linda Lee today is a 37-year-old, successful veterinarian with four children, three of whom are triplets. She is a living testimony of God's response to the prayers of His children. By His loving grace, God brought Linda Lee from the threshold of death to life in Jesus Christ.

My daughter's scars speak of the healing that comes from the wounds of God's Son. When I see her scars, I think of the shame Jesus endured. Because He endured the taunts of men without sinning, Linda Lee's shame—through faith—is erased.

When I see her scars, I think of the rejection Jesus endured. Because He endured the rejection of men without sinning, Linda Lee's rejection is erased. I also think of the death Jesus endured. Because He endured death on the Cross without sinning, Linda Lee will never die.

Because Jesus's hands are nail scarred, one day Linda Lee's will be smoother than silk. When I see her scars, I think of His scars, and I rejoice.

☀ ☀ ☀

SINGING IN CHAINS

To one degree or another, we all find ourselves dealing with difficult situations, sometimes beyond our control. Acts 16:23–40 tells the story of Paul and Silas and how they dealt with tough circumstances.

After being arrested, stripped, and beaten, Paul and Silas were thrown into prison.

"Guard these men carefully," was the order given to the jailer. So he placed them in the inner prison—a dark, damp dungeon, infested with rats and foul smells. And in this place hopelessness hung over the jail cells like a poisonous cloud. For prisoners who were there before Paul and Silas, life had been reduced to utter despair.

Yet, at midnight from the cell of Paul and Silas came songs, prayers, and praises to God. Can't you imagine the wonder of it all?

Other prisoners perhaps thought they were dreaming or delusional. Their minds must have pondered, *Are not these men also in chains and shackles? Yet, they are singing!*

Suddenly, a low rumble rattled the iron doors, and the earth began to shake violently. Then the doors to the prison cells burst open, and all the prisoners' chains came loose.

Startled awake, the jailer saw all the prison doors open and feared the prisoners had escaped. This meant imprisonment and death for him. Rather than face dying in disgrace, he drew his sword to kill himself.

> But Paul shouted, "Don't harm yourself! We are all here!"
>
> The jailer called for lights, rushed in and fell trembling before Paul and Silas. He then brought them out and asked, "Sirs, what must I do to be saved?"
>
> They replied, "Believe in the Lord Jesus, and you will be saved—you and your household." Then they spoke the word of the Lord to him and all the others in the house. At that hour of the night the jailer took them and washed their wounds; then immediately he and all his family were baptized. The jailer brought them into his house and set a meal before them; he was filled with joy because he had come to believe in God—he and his whole family.
>
> —Acts 16: 28–34

Just as Paul and Silas demonstrated a faith that changed lives and set men free, God enables those who have suffered great loss and grief to find hope and new beginnings. The chains that have bound our hearts and minds are removed, and in our new freedom we become Christ's ambassadors whose stories can touch lives and bring deeper understanding.

Deanna turned her brother's tragic death into a nationwide prison ministry, providing healing and hope for those who are often forgotten.

Remembering E. J.

Deanna Allen

"Deanna," my husband said over the phone, "you need to go to your mom's right away."

I knew it had something to do with my brother, E. J., who was in prison. Deep inside, I had a foreboding that this day in June would change our lives forever.

When I arrived at the house, our family attorney greeted me at the door. She said, "It's your brother—they found him dead. He left a note."

My mind swirled. *No, this can't be true! Not now, not when he finally had everything to live for. How could this happen?*

The attorney put her hand on my shoulder and continued, "Deanna, please see if you can calm your mom down. She is not dealing with the situation well."

I nodded and walked into her bedroom. Sitting down next to Mom, I put my arms around her. We cried together. I prayed silently that my family would survive this horrific ordeal.

Just before nine in the morning the next day, we received a call from the prison. We were told that an investigation of E. J.'s death would be conducted.

There were so many questions that no one seemed to be able to answer. If this tragedy had occurred the last time E. J. was in prison, I wouldn't have been surprised. But this time he'd worked so hard to change himself, and he'd become someone to be proud of.

He told us, "I'm not a loser anymore." He had a job he'd taken to heart. And E. J. only had nine more days before he'd be released. He was coming home to a new life and had plans to get married. There had been no signs or warnings.

Part of me slipped into a safe place—denial. I just knew someone from the prison would call and say it was a mistake— that someone else had died. But that didn't happen.

The following days and weeks went by in a blur. This was not the first time life had dealt me lemons, and in the past, God had turned them into lemonade. I prayed He'd do the same with this tragedy. I turned to Him for guidance. I remembered that once E. J. was called forward at a church event and told, "Your life is going to be like a star that will shine light on many lives." Was there a way this could still happen?

Ironically, I had just completed my book, *Pathway to Serenity: Overcoming Spiritual Bankruptcy.* It was written to set prisoners free and to bring them hope. Although it came too late to help E. J., I dedicated the book to him. I didn't understand why this had happened to E. J., but I sensed God had a plan. As I gave the situation over to Him, I saw the potential of my brother's life and story being told to help save other prisoners. A new fire grew inside me, not only to put the book into the hands of inmates, but to actually go and speak to them.

As time passed, this new purpose directed my path. My passion became clear: to share with prisoners the same hope, peace, and transformation I had found years before. Thus began the season of my life as national director of Daughters of Destiny prison ministry.

It's been three years now, and while I still miss E. J. very much, I know his life and death weren't wasted. Every prison or jail I go into I share his story, and it continues to bring a sobering reality to thousands. We only have today. There is no promise of tomorrow. We all have choices laid before us, and I urge those to whom I speak: "Choose life."

Had I been given a choice, I would have written this chapter of my family's life differently. But I will spend the rest of my life savoring this lemonade and remembering my brother as I go into jails and prisons just like where he died.

If I could tell E. J. anything, it would be that the story of his life is a shining light for many lives today—just not like I originally imagined.

☀ ☀ ☀

Words from Jeenie

There seemed to be no signs or warnings of E. J.'s impending death. Even as a professional, it is not always easy to pick up. As related in a previous chapter, our group of therapists did not detect our MD colleague was going to end his life, even though we knew he had struggled with depression. Suicide can be mystifying to family and friends.

Even in the aftermath of suicide, Deanna and her mother remembered the good things in E. J.'s life—a major way to start living again.

Many ministries have sprung from devastating, painful life experiences, as did Deanna's. God has used her suffering to touch the lives of many.

In the next story God reminds Beverly that He is with her every step of the way.

Pennies from Heaven
Beverly Henderson

My life changed forever on December 16, 2004—the day my husband of 32 years took his own life. The details of that day and the days to follow are forever etched in my memory.

Jimmy never let anyone know of his inner turmoil, depression, and chronic pain. He was a generous, kindhearted, compassionate man. After Jimmy died, my sister spoke of his quiet kindness and of how many people's lives had been touched in some way just because they knew him. She also reminded us that he had a heart for God. Even though, in this case, he acted outside God's will, we knew that God's love and compassion rested on him.

Over the Thanksgiving holiday, just three weeks prior to his death, Jimmy went to Oklahoma to visit our daughter, her husband, and our two precious granddaughters. I stayed at home because I had responsibilities at our church that weekend. As we were leaving to go to the airport, he bent down and picked up a shiny penny from the ground.

"Here," he said, "this penny means that from now on everything is going to be fine." He had been depressed, but it seemed things were turning around for him. He was seeking professional help, and he was the happiest I had seen him in years.

After his death, I gave each of our three daughters some of their dad's ashes so they could scatter them in their own special places. Imagine our amazement when we discovered a burned penny mixed in with the ashes. I smiled through my tears as I remembered the day Jimmy picked up the penny and told me everything was going to be fine.

The day after his memorial service, I went to his office to take care of a few things. I parked in his parking space, and as I got out of the car, I saw a shiny penny on the ground. Again, I was reminded that everything was going to be fine.

On Christmas Day, my girls filled a stocking for me, a random stocking they found in a box of Christmas decorations. As I emptied everything out, a shiny penny fell out of the stocking. At first I thought my girls had put it in there, but as I witnessed the looks in their eyes, I knew they were surprised, too.

One of my daughters and her husband went out for a run that afternoon. When they came back in the house, they found a penny on the doorstep. Again a reminder. My girls were helping me clean out their dad's desk at work. You guessed it—only this time there were three pennies.

Later, I found a penny on the windowsill, a penny on the piano the first Sunday I went back to church, a penny on the sidewalk on one particular day that I was feeling very low. I can honestly go on and on.

I realized one day that I was constantly looking down at the ground, looking for pennies. It occurred to me that I should look up. These pennies are there for me as a reminder that God is with me during every step of this journey of grief, and all I have to do is trust Him, and He will carry me through.

My favorite Scripture passage is Philippians 4:6–9, 13.

Do not be anxious about anything, but in everything, by prayer and petition, with thanksgiving, present your requests to God. And the peace of God, which transcends all understanding, will guard your hearts and your minds in Christ Jesus.

Finally, brothers, whatever is true, whatever is noble, whatever is right, whatever is pure, whatever is lovely, whatever is admirable—if anything is excellent or praiseworthy—think about such things. Whatever you have learned or received or heard from me, or seen in me—put it into practice. And the God of peace will be with you . . .

I can do everything through him who gives me strength.

I held on to God's promise of peace and strength, and I shall continue to do so. And I know I will be just fine.

☀ ☀ ☀

Words from Jeenie

During one dark, painful period of my life, my only hope was in the Lord. I did not know what the outcome would be, but underneath the torment, I was certain I was in His hands and under His control.

I realized it is through those days of anguish we learn our most precious lessons. Thus, I penned the following words:

I'll Exchange

Illusive happiness for indescribable peace,
Empty success for the lessons in defeat,
Overpowering sunlight for refreshing rain,
Majestic mountains for valleys,
Comfort for the growth in pain,
Because
I'm willing to trust You—
in my defeat,
during the rain of life, and
through my dark valleys.

"Do not grieve, for the joy of the Lord is your strength."
—Nehemiah 8:10

Our prayer is that this book has helped you as you grieve the loss of a loved one to suicide or deal with the pain of attempted suicide. We pray that you will also seek out caring family, friends, and a local church body to support you in this journey. Christian counseling services are also available in most communities. We pray you will find the joy of the Lord as your strength.

Reflections

1. Write down emotions that have kept you imprisoned. Then pray for release.

2. Visualize the chains that bind your heart falling off. Then believe that you are set free.

Prayer

Lord, thank You for giving me the strength to go on with my life. Facing the truth has set me free. Help me to show others grace and mercy. Let my life be an example by the wholeness and renewal You've brought back into my life. In Jesus's name I pray, amen.

SUICIDE:
FACTS AND
RESOURCES

NATIONAL

- Every day approximately 90 Americans take their own life, and 2,300 more attempt to do so.

- Suicide is the fourth leading cause of death for adults between the ages of 18 and 65 years in the United States, with 27,321 suicides among that age group.

- There are four male suicides for every one female suicide, but three times as many females as males attempt suicide.

- In 2006 (most recent data available), a total of 33,300 deaths by suicide were reported in the United States.

Source: National Center for Health Statistics, 2006

INTERNATIONAL

- In the year 2000, approximately 1 million people died from suicide: a global mortality rate of 16 per 100,000, or one death every 40 seconds.

- It is estimated that there are up to 20 times as many suicide attempts as suicide deaths.

- In the last 45 years suicide rates have increased by 60 percent worldwide.

Source: World Health Organization. Most recent statistics available, www.who.int/mental_health/prevention/suicide/suicideprevent/en/index.html, accessed August 2009.

These figures are available from the American Foundation for Suicide Prevention, www.afsp.org. Check the Web site for updated information, resources, and support networks.

Resources

Did You Know?

⇨ You can dial 211 or go to www.211.org for help in locating essential community services, such as mental and health services. This service is available for 39 states, the District of Columbia, and Puerto Rico.

⇨ You can call the National Suicide Prevention Lifeline at 1-800-273-TALK (8255), a free, 24-hour hotline available to anyone in suicidal crisis or emotional distress. Your call will be routed to the nearest crisis center to you.

⇨ You can also dial the following National Suicide Prevention Hotline numbers operated by the Substance Abuse and Mental Health Services Administration of the Department of Health and Human Services:

- 1-800-SUICIDE (1-800-784-2433)
- 1-888-SUICIDE (1-888-784-2433)
- 1-877-SUICIDA (1-877-784-2432) (Spanish).

⇨ You can search a directory of Christian counselors through the National Christian Counselors Association at http://www.ncca.org/Directory/.

⇨ You can contact the ministry of Focus on the Family any time at 1-800-A-Family (232-6459).

New Hope Publishers and the authors cannot warrant or endorse the resources listed above.

The contact information listed is correct as of August 2009. Readers are encouraged to seek assistance from Christian ministers, counselors, and trained lay leaders.

New Hope® Publishers is a division of WMU®, an international organization that challenges Christian believers to understand and be radically involved in God's mission. For more information about WMU, go to www.wmu.com. More information about New Hope books may be found at www.newhopepublishers.com. New Hope books may be purchased at your local bookstore.

If you've been blessed by this book, we would like to hear your story. The publisher and author welcome your comments and suggestions at: newhopereader@wmu.org.

Other New Hope Books

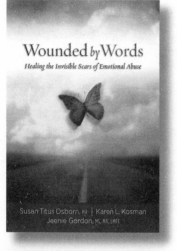

Wounded by Words
*Healing the Invisible Scars
of Emotional Abuse*
Susan Titus Osborn, Karen L.
Kosman, and Jeenie Gordon
ISBN-10: 1-59669-049-6
ISBN-13: 978-1-59669-049-3

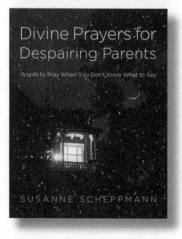

Divine Prayers
for Despairing Parents
*Words to Pray When You
Don't Know What to Say*
Susanne Scheppmann
ISBN-10: 1-59669-206-5
ISBN-13: 978-1-59669-206-0

Available in bookstores everywhere

For information about these books or any New Hope product,
visit www.newhopepublishers.com.